MARKETING

An International Perspective

Irwin Perspectives in International Business

Series Coeditors
James E. Harf   *The Ohio State University*
Robert R. Miller   *University of Houston*
B. Thomas Trout   *University of New Hampshire*

MARKETING

An International Perspective

Philip R. Cateora
University of Colorado

Susan M. Keaveney
University of Denver

1987

Homewood, Illinois 60430

To:
John, Virginia, Joanne, Kass,
Nancy, Deborah, Phyllis, and Hank

ISBN 0-256-05626-9

Library of Congress Catalog Card No. 86-83392

Printed in the United States of America

3 4 5 6 7 8 9 0 E 4 3 2 1 0 9 8 7

PREFACE

Marketing: An International Perspective is one of a series of six volumes produced under the direction of the Consortium for International Studies Education with support from the U.S. Department of Education. The specific aim of the series is to provide an international dimension for the core functional courses in business administration for colleges and universities. The first four volumes are intended to be used in conjunction with introductory textbooks in accounting, finance, management, and marketing. The other two books provide supplemental material for the introduction to business course; the first discusses international environmental matters, while the second addresses managerial issues. Books in the series have been tailored to supplement individual chapters in many of the leading textbooks in the core areas covered.

Each volume was produced under the general direction of a team leader. In most cases this leader also coauthored the respective area book. Team leaders were:

Accounting:	Professor Gerhard G. Mueller, University of Washington
Finance:	Professor Arthur I. Stonehill, Oregon State University
Management:	Professor R. Hal Mason, University of California, Los Angeles
Marketing:	Professor Philip R. Cateora, University of Colorado
Introduction to Business:	Professor Robert R. Miller, University of Houston–University Park

Each of these leaders has authored or coauthored leading international textbooks in their areas of scholarly expertise. Each has also produced numerous technical articles. Volumes in this series and their authors are:

Accounting: An International Perspective, by Gerhard G. Mueller, Helen Gernon (University of Oregon), and Gary Meek (Oklahoma State University).

Finance: An International Perspective, by Arthur I. Stonehill and David K. Eiteman (UCLA).

Management: An International Perspective, by R. Hal Mason and Robert Spich (UCLA).

Marketing: An International Perspective, by Philip R. Cateora (University of Colorado–Boulder) and Susan M. Keaveney (University of Denver).

Introduction to Business: An International Perspective, by Robert R. Miller, and Janice J. Miller (University of Houston–University Park).

Issues for Managers: An International Perspective, by John A. Kilpatrick (University of Northern Colorado) and Janice J. Miller.

Codirectors of the project for the Consortium were James E. Harf (The Ohio State University), Robert R. Miller, and B. Thomas Trout (University of New Hampshire).

Department of Education sponsorship of this project was a part of its efforts to expand international awareness in U.S. higher education. In this regard, the Department's interests coincided with those of the American Assembly of Collegiate Schools of Business (AACSB), which recently included internationalization of curricula as a requirement for accreditation of American college and university degree programs in business administration. This emphasis by AACSB is likely to be strengthened in coming years, and the series of which this volume is a part is dedicated specifically to satisfying the AACSB mandate.

Marketing: An International Perspective is designed to accompany introductory marketing textbooks to provide an international curriculum dimension. Its organization reflects the customary flow of topics presented in required courses in marketing. The first chapter presents an overview of the internationalization of the American market and illustrates the differences that need to be addressed when a company becomes international. The next chapter explores the environmental uncontrollables confronting the marketer when doing business in foreign countries. This is followed by chapters on marketing research, product development, pricing, distribution, and promotion. The differences that may occur when marketing internationally are stressed throughout the text. A final chapter presents an in-depth treatment of topics that pervade the international environment and which can impact the success of international marketing operations. These topics also reflect issues with which today's business students should be conversant.

The text is designed to stimulate a curiosity in international issues that affect management practices of companies seeking market opportunities outside the United States. A primary objective is to raise the student's consciousness of the importance of viewing business operations from a worldwide perspective.

Acknowlegments

The authors and the Consortium gratefully acknowledge the support of the Department of Education for this project. In addition, many individuals made significant contributions. Gail McCutcheon, of The Ohio State University, assisted in field testing. Steven Garrett, Troy State University, Jerome Guffy, Humbolt State College, Dennis Guseman, California State College—Bakersfield, and Allan C. Reddy, Valdosta State College tested versions of the manuscript in their respective classes during the fall of 1985. We wish to acknowledge the helpful assistance of the students and professors who completed evaluations and furnished the authors with invaluable feedback.

Philip R. Cateora
Boulder, Colorado
Susan Keaveney
Denver, Colorado

CONTENTS

Deciding to Conduct Primary Research. Conducting International
Marketing Research. Summary.

CHAPTER ONE

International Marketing—What Is It?

International marketing, once a topic of interest only to those few students who sought careers in international business, is now a subject with which every business student, regardless of career goals, should be familiar. The international economic interdependence of the United States and American businesses makes it necessary to study business from a global perspective to ensure an inclusive business preparation.

Just a few short years ago most products sold in the United States were American-made, and the majority of American firms operated only within the United States. Today, a high percentage of U.S. firms are involved to some degree in foreign markets. U.S. consumers spend their dollars for products from all over the world; we are all familiar with Toyota, Sony, Volkswagen, and other foreign-made goods which compete for the American consumer's dollar. The trend is for markets throughout the world to be sought after by businesses from many countries. Indications are that competition for world markets will continue to intensify, thus decreasing the number of companies that operate solely in domestic markets.

Those of you preparing for business careers need to be conversant with the techniques of doing business internationally whether or not you are seeking an international job.

Even though you may never be employed in an international division of a company, or the company for whom you work may not be engaged in business outside the United States, you still need to be aware of the problems and processes of international business so you can understand today's business environment and the problems of your customers who are involved in international business. In short, to understand business at almost any level you must be knowledgeable about both domestic and international activities. The extent of internationalization of business today is only the beginning of the eventual globalization of all businesses, large or small, that will occur during your business careers. Not to be knowledgeable about international business is to be undereducated in today's business world. Let us look more closely at some of the conditions in the marketplace that make an understanding of international business imperative for a well-educated business person.

THE INTERNATIONALIZATION OF THE U.S. ECONOMY

The internationalization of the American economy has accelerated during the last decade. Indications for the future point to our becoming more economically interdependent with the rest of the world, and therefore more dependent on international trade. Increasing demand for diminishing sources of energy, fluctuating exchange rates, balance of trade surpluses and deficits, influence of world petroleum prices by OPEC, different rates of economic growth, varying levels of inflation, emergence of the Third World as an important economic force, and declining raw material reserves are all examples of conditions producing a new world economic interdependence of which the United States is a part.

We are all familiar with the United States' dependence on foreign sources of petroleum and the omnipresent Japanese automobile, but there are other trends that are equally important. During the last two decades, for example, there has been a significant increase in the importance of exports to our economy; a variety of foreign products have earned a significant share of U.S. markets; foreign companies make substantial investments in the United States; there has been a major increase in foreign ownership or control of familiar U.S. businesses; foreign investment by U.S. firms and their dependence on foreign earnings has been increasing; and competition for world markets is intensifying. Let us examine each of these trends more closely.

Increase in U.S. Exports

The first important trend in the internationalization of the U.S. economy has been the extent to which U.S. companies have become involved in exporting. Between 1975 and 1985 total U.S. production of manufactured goods increased by 57 percent while exports of manufactured goods from the United States increased by 127 percent. According to the Treasury Department exports accounted for one out of every nine manufacturing jobs in the United States in 1985. In agriculture, farm production increased between 1975 and 1985 by 68 percent but agricultural exports increased 198 percent, accounting for one out of every three jobs in agriculture. It is estimated that there are over 40,000 firms in the United States directly involved in exporting or which have business investments abroad. Today, one out of every three dollars of U.S. corporate profits is derived from the international activity of U.S. firms.

Increase in Foreign Imports

While U.S. companies have been exporting at an increasing rate, foreign firms have been busy in American markets. In a number of product categories, foreign firms control a significant share of the U.S. market. Over 70 percent of all color televisions sold in the United States are manufactured by foreign firms; foreign-made automobiles have increased their market share from a little more than 4 percent in 1960 to over 30 percent today. Foreign companies also have important market positions in such product categories as radios, stereos, office machinery, and clothing. Similar foreign competition exists for industrial goods as well; as an example, 40 percent of all machine tools sold in the United States are imported, and most aircraft used by U.S. commuter airlines are foreign made.

Foreign Investment in the United States

Many foreign companies have made significant investments in the United States. Honda (Japan) manufactures automobiles here, Renault (France) owns a significant share of American Motors Company. Nestle (Switzerland) owns Libby (the food processor), and Keebler Cookies is a British firm. Foreign companies invest in United States corporations in two ways: (1) by buying part or all of an already existing company, as was the case when Nestle bought Libby, or (2) by establishing subsidiaries, such as Sony Corporation of America. Foreign ownership or control of U.S. business is a major phenomenon of the 1970s and 80s.

Foreign investment in U.S. companies has resulted in such well-known American brand names as French's mustard, Peter Paul candy bars, Clorox bleach, Capitol Records, and Foster Grant sunglasses being either owned or controlled by foreign corporations. In addition, such well-known retailers as Saks Fifth Avenue (France), A & P (Germany), and Grand Union (Great Britain) grocery stores are partially or 100 percent foreign owned.

U.S. Investment Abroad

While foreign firms have been effectively competing for U.S. markets, U.S. firms have been actively pursuing markets outside the United

States. As already mentioned, one out of every three dollars of U.S. corporate profits is derived from foreign earnings; these profits come from export sales and investments abroad. Earnings from foreign sales are an important source of income for many American companies. The Black & Decker Corporation has reported as much as 70 percent of their total earnings were generated by foreign sales and investments; Johnson & Johnson has reported 51 percent, Revlon 23 percent, F. W. Woolworth Co. 59 percent, and Avon Products 38 percent. Coca-Cola, Gillette, and Firestone, with earnings generated by foreign sales of 57 percent, 60 percent, and 83 percent respectively, have been involved in international business for decades. Other companies such as Mattel, Revlon, and Campbell Soup Company have "gone international" only within the last few decades.

Competition Intensifies in World Markets

U.S. firms not only face strong foreign competition for U.S. markets, they also face increasing competition for markets outside the United States. Competition for world markets comes from industrialized countries such as Japan, Germany, and France as well as from newly industrialized countries (NICs) like Korea, Brazil, Mexico, Hong Kong, and Singapore. (The NICs frequently specialize in single industries and operate with the full economic support of their governments.) Brazil, considered a developing country, is an important market for many U.S. products but, at the same time, competes against U.S. companies with Brazilian-made products both within the U.S. market as well as in other foreign markets. Brazil exports, annually, over a billion dollars of technologically advanced products ranging from high-performance pistons for U.S. aircraft engines to commuter aircraft. In fact, 75 percent of the market for commuter aircraft in the United States is controlled by Brazil, Canada, and Ireland. Brazil also produces Volkswagens that compete in the Latin American automobile market with U.S.- and Japanese-made autos.

In summary, U.S. businesses face competition at home from foreign imports and from foreign firms who control U.S. companies. In foreign markets they face competition from other industrialized nations as well as companies from emerging countries.

Based on this discussion, the conclusion which must be drawn is that any individual whose career is not influenced by international business will be in the minority. Even though you may not be employed by a firm that is exporting, you most likely will do business with firms that are. In your business career, it is unlikely you will escape involvement with international business.

Before we go further, perhaps we need to explore some of the ideas and concepts associated with international business. What is international business? International marketing? Are there real differences between international business and domestic business? If so, what are those differences and how do you adjust to them?

DOMESTIC AND INTERNATIONAL BUSINESS: WHAT IS THE DIFFERENCE?

The goal of business is to satisfy the wants and needs of consumers by promoting, pricing, and distributing products for which there is a market. The purpose of business is the same whether it is conducted in the smallest community in the United States or anywhere else in the world. If the purpose of business is the same everywhere in the world, then what is the difference between international and domestic business?

International Businesses Operate in More Than One Country

Domestic business is conducted solely within the home country, while international business is conducted in more than one country. The international activity may be as basic as exporting to one customer in another country or as involved as manufacturing and marketing several products in several different countries. Companies that only export products from their home country are generally called exporters, international exporters, or foreign exporters. Companies that manufacture and sell products in many different countries are known as international, transnational, or multinational enterprises (MNEs), or multinational companies (MNCs). Regardless of the name given a company engaged in foreign business, a company that does business in more than one country is correctly said to be in international business.

International Businesses Respond to More Than One Uncontrollable Environment

International businesses operate across national borders and must, therefore, respond to environmental forces within each of the foreign nations in which they do business. A domestic company reacts only to its home environment; an international business must react not only to its domestic environment but to the environment within each of the countries in which it operates.

A company's environment consists of all the forces that influence the activities and success of a firm. The marketing mix (product, price, promotion, and distribution), the controllable part of a company's environment, is determined by management when the company decides what product it will produce, what price it will charge, how it will be distributed, and how it will be promoted. There are an infinite variety of combinations of the controllable elements that can constitute a marketing mix.

Once implemented, every marketing mix is influenced by a variety of environmental elements over which management has no direct control. Any external force not governed by the company but which influences the outcome of its efforts is an uncontrollable element. Some of the more obvious uncontrollable elements of an environment are:

Culture	Competition
Politics	Economics
Legal restrictions	Technology
Sociology	Distribution
Geography	Labor

An astute marketer anticipates the influences of these uncontrollable elements and adapts a company's market mix accordingly.

Adaptation is as necessary in international marketing as it is in domestic marketing. The difference for the international marketer is that the product may have to be adapted to multiple foreign environments in addition to the company's home environment. A business does not escape the influences of the home country uncontrollables just because it does business in another country.

Home Country Uncontrollables Influence International Plans.
The influence of home country uncontrollables remains constant regardless of how many countries a company does business in. For example, most of the world's countries require a citizen to have its government's permission to trade with another country. National security and domestic economic policies are major reasons for controlling trade: War or other hostilities between nations can cause trade to be restricted for strategic reasons; if another country's trade policies are judged discriminatory or unfair, trade may be restricted in retaliation; and exporting scarce goods may be prohibited in order to conserve them. On the other hand, if the home country's economy needs stimulation, inducements to engage in business abroad frequently are provided in order to keep manufacturing plants operating. In addition to the legal and economic reasons for constraining trade, other uncontrollables such as labor politics, competition, and available resources may influence the way a company is permitted to do business abroad. When going international a company's marketing mix must be adapted to the influences of the home country uncontrollables. As a company moves into

an international market, the process of adaptation is further complicated by the differences between home country and foreign country
uncontrollables.

Foreign Environmental Elements Have Different Meanings.

Adaptation becomes more complex in international marketing because
each of the uncontrollable elements in each environment can have a
different impact. Even though foreign and home market environmental
components (i.e., legal, cultural, economic, etc.) are the same, their
substance and, thus, effect can be quite different and frequently unfamiliar to management. For example, a Westerner must learn that
white, not black, is the symbol of mourning in parts of the Far East,
quite different from our Western culture where white symbolizes pu-
rity, as with a bridal gown. The use of the number four in Japan should
be avoided since the word for four, *shi,* is also the Japanese word for
death. Both of these examples arise from the cultural element of the
environment, both show how meanings differ from country to country.
The differences in foreign uncontrollables and our unfamiliarity with
them are the basis for the differences between domestic and international business.

Multiple Environments Confront the Decision Maker.

As a com-
pany moves from a domestic to a foreign market, the process of adaptation becomes more complex because of the addition of the several
sets of foreign uncontrollables. Consider the countless problems generated for a decision maker by multiple sets of environmental forces
with different meanings for each foreign market a company adds to
its marketing plan. One example of the impact of diversity in multiple
markets is illustrated by the problems of a cake mix manufacturer.
When cake mixes were first introduced in the United States, the marketer had problems overcoming the housewife's guilt feelings associated with "instant, prepared" foods. The same cake mix in England
was rejected because most English did not eat the traditional American
"iced cakes" but preferred tea cakes closely resembling plain sponge
cakes. When the same cake mix was introduced in Japan, it produced
yet a different problem; the housewife was concerned about failing.
She wanted the cake mix to be as complete and fail-safe as possible.
To assure the Japanese housewife that "success" was possible, the company stressed in their advertisements that "making a cake from a cake
mix was as easy as making rice." While this seemed logical to the
American marketer who viewed making rice, a staple in the Japanese
diet, as easy for the Japanese cook, it offended the Japanese housewife
who believed that making rice required great skill. Since the cake mix
was equated with rice making, the Japanese housewife felt it had a

high potential for failure. In all three environments, the cake mix company just wanted to sell cake mixes, but each environment posed a different cultural problem of adaptation.

Difficult to Assess Impact of Environmental Elements

The impact of the foreign environment is not only different but it frequently changes abruptly, and its importance is often difficult to assess. Information may not be available, and/or the quality of data may not be adequate to measure the impact on a marketing mix.

Political attitudes, for example, can change dramatically and almost overnight, and laws unfriendly to foreign companies can be passed that will alter a marketing program's success. The Indian government ordered the Coca-Cola Company to disclose its secret formula for Coca-Cola in order to continue to do business in India. Coke refused and was not allowed to continue selling Coke in India, a potential market of over 700 million people. Could Coke have anticipated such an abrupt change in the law? Perhaps, but such forecasting of change in environmental components is, at best, a very difficult and complicated task.

Even when a marketer realizes that environmental components are different, the ability to assess those differences may be difficult because of a lack of information. The market data that U.S. businesses are accustomed to are not available in many countries or, if available, these data are frequently inaccurate. A population census, an important statistic for innumerable marketing decisions, can be out of date and therefore inaccurate. The last time a population census was taken in Bolivia was 1950, and in the People's Republic of China over 30 years passed between census dates, 1953–84. Economic reports and production figures so readily available about U.S. businesses are frequently unavailable or improperly compiled in many countries. For each foreign market there is a set of uncontrollable elements that influence the success of a company's marketing mix. However, before you can adapt to the environment you must be aware of the need for adaptation; the assessment of these needs is the basis for the study of international marketing.

The need to adapt to both home country and host country environmental constraints is the essential difference between domestic and international business. Most failures in international business stem from ineffective adaptation of the marketing mix to the constraints imposed by foreign uncontrollables. The influence of uncontrollables is either ignored, assumed to be the same as in the home country, or improperly evaluated as to its impact on the marketing mix; in short, it is a failure to adapt. For these reasons, uncontrollables will be emphasized throughout the text, particularly in Chapter 2 where uncontrollables will be discussed in some detail.

SELF-REFERENCE CRITERION—OBSTACLE TO EFFECTIVE ADAPTATION

The key to successful international business is adaptation to the differences in the environment that usually exist from one market to another. Adaptation is not a passive process but a conscious effort on the part of the international marketer to anticipate the influences of both the foreign and domestic uncontrollable environments on a marketing mix and then to adjust the marketing mix to minimize their effects. One authority suggests that the primary obstacle to success in international business is a person's self-reference criterion (SRC) in making decisions, that is, an unconscious reference to one's own cultural values, experiences, and knowledge as a basis for decisions. The SRC impedes the ability to assess a foreign market in its true light.

When confronted with a set of facts, we react spontaneously on the basis of knowledge accumulated over a lifetime. We seldom stop to think about a reaction, we simply react. Thus, when faced with a problem in another culture, the tendency is to react instinctively and refer to our SRC for a solution. Our reactions, however, are based on meanings, values, symbols, and behavior relevant to our own culture and frequently different from those of the foreign culture; such decisions are generally not valid.

To illustrate the impact of the SRC, consider the misunderstanding that can occur as the result of what is felt to be "personal space" between people of different cultures. In the United States unrelated individuals keep a certain physical distance between themselves when talking or standing in line. We do not consciously think about that distance; we know what it is without thinking—we are relying on our SRC. When someone gets too close we immediately feel uncomfortable and back away. In some cultures the acceptable distance between individuals is substantially less than in the United States. So, when a U.S. citizen, unaware of another culture's acceptable distances, is approached too closely by a foreigner, the American unconsciously reacts by backing away to restore proper distance (i.e., proper in American culture). Confusion results for both parties. The American immediately assumes the foreigner is pushy, while the foreigner assumes the American is unfriendly and standoffish. By each reacting to the values of his/her own SRC, both are victims of a cultural misunderstanding.

Your SRC can prevent you from being aware that there are cultural differences or from recognizing the real importance of those differences.

Thus, you either fail to recognize the need to take action, or you discount the cultural differences that exist among countries. In the opinion of the authors, understanding and dealing with the self-reference criterion is one of the more important facets in international business.

This phenomenon influences the evaluation of the appropriateness of a domestically designed marketing mix for a foreign market. If the U.S. marketer is not careful, he/she may evaluate the marketing mix on U.S. experiences (i.e., his/her SRC) without fully appreciating the importance of the cultural differences that require adaptation. Nova, a type of Chevrolet, is a successful name in the United States and would seem harmless enough for foreign countries; however, in Spanish *no va* means *won't go,* hardly a desirable image for an automobile. Another example is Cue toothpaste. The name seems like a good one for that product, yet in French-speaking countries *cue* is a crude slang expression for derriere; not the image the company had in mind for its toothpaste. Both of these examples of real mistakes made by major companies stem from relying on the SRC in making a decision. In the U.S. culture a person's SRC would not reveal any problem with either *Nova* or *Cue,* but in international marketing relying on one's SRC can mean an inadequately adapted marketing program ending in failure.

RAISING YOUR CULTURAL AWARENESS AND SENSITIVITY

A. major step in controlling the influence of the SRC is recognizing its existence in our behavior. While it is impossible for someone to learn every culture in-depth and to be aware of all the important differences, an awareness of the need to be sensitive to differences and to ask questions when doing business with another culture can prevent many of the mistakes of international business. In the following chapters we will discuss further how to control the SRC when the elements of the uncontrollable environment of international marketing are presented.

ORIENTATION OF MARKETING—A GLOBAL PERSPECTIVE

The orientation of this text can best be described as an international, environmental approach to marketing. By no means is it intended to present principles of marketing; rather, it is intended to demonstrate some of the unique problems that arise when companies market across national boundaries. It attempts to relate the influence of the foreign environment to the marketing process and, thus, illustrate the many ways in which the environment affects the marketing task. Although marketing principles are universally applicable, the environment within which the marketer must implement marketing plans changes drastically from country to country. It is with the difficulties created by different environments that this text is primarily concerned.

The environmental approach of *Marketing: An International Perspective* permits a truly worldwide orientation. The reader's horizons are not limited to any specific nation and its particular way of doing business. Instead, the book provides readers with an approach and framework with which to identify and analyze the important environmental uniqueness of each nation or region. In the authors' opinion, the key to successful international marketing is adaptation—adaptation to an ever-changing, mostly uncontrollable, and to the inexperienced, frequently incomprehensible environment. Success most often hinges on the ability to assess and adjust properly to the impact of a strange environment.

The first section of *Marketing: An International Perspective* offers a view of the world as a market including an in-depth look at the uncontrollable environmental elements and their assessment. The next section deals exclusively with the problems of adapting a marketing mix to world markets, with a final section on future changes in the marketplace as the world becomes increasingly more economically interdependent. In each chapter the impact of the environment on the marketing process is illustrated.

As you read this text, look for several key points to help you develop a worldwide orientation. A primary objective of the text is to raise the reader's consciousness of the importance of culture to marketing, so, when confronted with the task of marketing in a foreign milieu, the impact of crucial cultural issues will not be overlooked.

As you read each chapter look for cultural differences between your country's culture and other cultures. Try to determine how those differences may affect a company's marketing program. Also, try to identify ways your SRC could lead you to incorrect action if you were not aware of the importance of cultural differences in marketing.

In addition, identify those principles, terms, concepts, and institutions of marketing that are unique to international marketing (there are not many) and those principles, terms, concepts, and institutions that need to be extended to cover experiences in international marketing.

EXERCISE 1–1

We all know about Japanese automobiles and televisions, but what other goods do we buy that are either foreign made or from a company that is owned by a foreign multinational? After you complete this exercise, you might just be surprised by how international your purchases are.

For one week, keep a list of all the products you use or buy each day that are foreign made or are purchased from foreign companies. The obvious things like automobiles and televisions will be easy to spot, but do not overlook the less obvious. For example, if you use any of the products from the companies listed below, you have purchased something from a company that is either totally owned or controlled by a foreign multinational.

Libby, McNeill & Libby (food processor)
Capitol Records (recorded music)
Bantam Books (paperback books)
Foster Grant (sunglasses)
Keebler Company (cookies)
Stouffer Foods (food processor)
Peter Paul (candy bars)

If you shop at Grand Union or Saks Fifth Avenue or spend the night at a Travelodge, you have done business with a non-U.S. firm.

ADDITIONAL READINGS

Cateora, Philip. *International Marketing.* 6th ed. Homewood, Ill.: Richard D. Irwin, 1987, Chs. 1–3.

Gall, Norman. "Black Ships Are Coming?" *Forbes,* January 31, 1983, pp. 67–75.

"Global Competition: The New Reality." *Europe Today,* Summer 1985, pp. 71–85.

Levitt, Theodore. "The Globalization of Markets." *Harvard Business Review,* May–June 1983, pp. 92–102.

Naisbitt, John. *Megatrends.* New York: Warner Books, 1982.

"Why Unilever Wants to Buy America." *Business Week,* October 21, 1985, p. 116.

Classics.   These are older but still very important sources for additional reading.

Bartels, Robert. *Global Development and Marketing.* Columbus, Ohio: Grid, 1981.

Lee, James A. "Cultural Analysis in Overseas Operations." *Harvard Business Review,* March–April 1966, pp. 106–11.

Environment of International Marketing

In Chapter 1 we introduced the concepts of controllable and uncontrollable elements in the international marketing environment. As you may recall, we began by stating that the objective of marketing is to satisfy the wants and needs of consumers. The marketing division of the firm performs that function by carefully planning and implementing the controllable elements of the marketing mix: product, price, promotion, and distribution. However, these activities do not take place in a vacuum; in fact, a number of uncontrollable elements influence marketing decisions. For the U.S. firm operating in the home market, *domestic uncontrollables* can include legal, governmental, political, and competitive influences. For the U.S. firm doing business internationally, the situation increases in complexity. The international marketer must consider the impact of *foreign uncontrollables,* such as the cultural, political, governmental, legal, economic, competitive, and technological environment of the host country. In this chapter we shall investigate in detail these issues that were raised in a broad sense in our introductory overview. The model that follows gives some idea of the environmental influences on the firm.

THE INTERNATIONAL MARKETING ENVIRONMENT

The first step in developing an international marketing plan is to research uncontrollable environmental situations, first in the home country and then in the host country. This research should provide sufficient information to identify potential barriers to doing business. If no insurmountable barriers are detected, the research on foreign uncontrollable elements will provide information that will be the basis

EXHIBIT 2–1   The International Marketing Environment

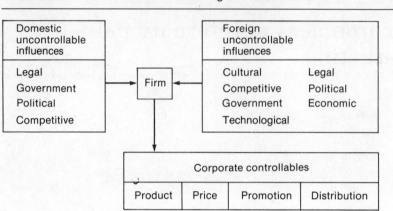

for decisions regarding the controllable elements—the marketing mix. Later chapters will discuss the impact of foreign uncontrollable elements on the marketing mix. This chapter will identify the various foreign uncontrollable elements, briefly review some of the kinds of information that should be gathered and the questions that should be asked, and conclude with examples of how these elements could influence international marketing.

CULTURE

Culture can be defined as the sum total of mankind's knowledge, beliefs, art, morals, laws, customs, and any other capabilities and habits acquired by humans as members of society. It is a group of people's distinctive way of life, their "design for living." With this extended definition we might include in our cultural analysis the political, legal, and economic areas, which follow later in this chapter. However, for our purposes we shall distinguish the last three factors as most often leading to mandatory changes in marketing and therefore as sources of potential trade barriers. Cultural factors on the other hand, such as aesthetics (art, music, dance, beauty), religion, education, social groups, technology, and language tend to require discretionary change, and may signal market barriers. Cultural factors may indicate that changes in the marketing mix should be implemented in order to increase the acceptance of the product in foreign markets and to further stimulate demand. However, these changes are made voluntarily by the international marketer in the hopes of greater success in meeting the needs of the target market, rather than at the mandate of the host country.

Aesthetics

This term refers to a culture's concept of beauty; it includes color, taste, art, dance, music, and theatre. Cultural aesthetic differences may affect product components, labels, trademarks, symbols, packaging, and product uses. For example, companies around the world have responded to differences in *tastes*. One soft drink company makes orange soda in 14 different flavors to please customers throughout the world. Many companies utilize local ingredients (for example, sweeteners, oils, flour) to adapt to local tastes. The Campbell Soup Company modifies its soup flavors, especially tomato: Irish and Italians want a creamy tomato soup; Germans want tomato with rice; and Colombians want a spicy tomato.[1]

Colors may have significantly different meanings as well. "Blue is for boys" in the United States, but red is the masculine color in France and England. Cultural musical differences may indicate changes in promotional themes. Pepsi-Cola adapted their "Come alive with Pepsi" TV commercials to fit North American, South American, and European audiences. Party scenes were changed to reflect the geography, local dress, racial characteristics, and activities of the local culture. The rock music in North America was changed to "bossa nova" in South America.

At other times, no change may be required. Cultural aesthetic universals may be discovered, for example, and utilized to the advantage of the marketer. Revlon has used a French producer to develop television commercials featuring Parisian scenes with English or Spanish language messages for international markets. Apparently the concept of beautiful Parisian women is global.[2]

Religion

The major religions of the world have a significant cultural impact, and in fact many times religion is the inner determinant of the external manifestations of culture. Educational systems, political and social organizations, family relationships, the role of women, and material values are often based on religious foundations. Because religion is often the source or center of culture, it can be useful in segmenting markets and in understanding consumer behavior. In addition it can be useful in understanding business customs and values.

One author makes the analogy between religion and economic development.[3] For example, Buddhism is more than just a religion in the

Western sense, but is a way of life for many people. It is considered by some to be a world-denying religion, which emphasizes asceticism and contemplation rather than consumption and work. Buddhist countries of Southeast Asia are all at the lower end of economic development. In contrast, the Protestant countries that value the "Protestant work ethic" are in the top levels of economic development. Religion can influence the way people feel about work and can affect the value placed on material goods.

Religion may also have specific taboos of which the marketer should be aware. Islam, for example, prohibits the drinking of alcohol and the eating of pork. In one case, a home appliance company thoughtlessly used a standard photograph of a refrigerator full of food to promote its product in the Middle East. The photograph featured a chunk of ham, centrally placed in the refrigerator. Needless to say the ad was considered insensitive and unappealing by the locals. In a more forceful example, one firm caused an international incident when its advertisements printed words across a picture of Buddha; this was considered disrespectful (at best). To safely avoid such blunders, marketers would be well advised to avoid the use of religious symbols in advertising.

Education

Levels of education vary greatly in the world, but it is safe to assume that the people in the MDCs (more developed countries) are more literate and better educated than those in the LDCs (less developed countries).* Well-educated consumers are better equipped to understand complex products; they can read instructions, labels, print advertisements, warranties, and they are likely to respond to rational promotional messages. The reverse is true for less-developed countries where illiteracy is widespread and consumers are not familiar with instructions or with product warranties. Nestle's unfortunate experience with uneducated consumers in LLDCs (least developed countries) is one example. The inability of LLDC consumers to understand the written instructions for Nestle baby formula led to the institution of requirements by many of these countries that product instructions be clearly illustrated.

---

*The authors use the standard United Nations (UN) classification system. The more-developed countries, or MDCs, include the United States, Canada, Australia and New Zealand, Japan, and most of Europe (particularly Western Europe). The less-developed countries, or LDCs, include much of South America, Africa, and Asia. The least developed countries, or LLDCs, are the underdeveloped nations of the world.

Social Groups

The roles that individuals play in a society and their relationships with one another also influence buying behavior. For example, the structure of the family unit differs from culture to culture. In the United States the family group is the nuclear family with one or two children and both parents in the work force. Also growing in importance are single parent households and single person households. The "traditional" U.S. family (with father in the work force, mother at home, and two children) now represents less than 7 percent of all U.S. households. In Latin America and the Middle East the extended family is the norm: Several nuclear families may live in one household. This makes it more difficult for the marketer to estimate household income and especially buying patterns. Who buys the product, who uses the product, who influences the purchase decision, and who makes the purchase decision may be difficult to ascertain. The husband/father in the Latin American family may authorize and pay for food purchases, but his decision will be influenced by his wife. The products will be consumed by the entire family, but physically purchased by a servant.

Individual family size also varies. In Europe and most MDCs, parents have one or two children; in Latin America they may have four or five children, while in Africa mothers still give birth to anywhere from six to nine children. This fact will certainly affect quantities purchased and packaging sizes. For example, Pillsbury's most popular package size in the United States provides two servings, while it packages in six- to eight-serving sizes for LDCs.[4] Yet one cannot assume that all package sizes sold in LDCs are large. Lack of income and the custom of daily purchases may mean that the most frequently purchased package sizes are small by U.S. standards. Razor blades are sold singly in some countries as are sticks of gum, and it is not unusual to see cigarettes sold in packs of four or five.

Social class is another cultural factor that influences consumer behavior. In some societies, class structure is clearly defined and carefully observed, such as the caste system in India. In other societies, class structure is more subtle, as in the United States. Regardless of the degree of structure, social class can influence product acceptance, promotional messages, and the relative importance of trademarks and brand names. In France, for example, for a product to gain widespread acceptance it must first succeed in Paris. Once the fashionable Parisian upper classes accept the product, the other social classes will follow suit. In another example, an American tea company tried unsuccessfully to market tea in India. Its advertisements targeted the wealthy upper class, who would have the income to buy this expensive imported tea. The advertisement showed an elite Indian family in an elegant home, with a beautiful silver tea service on the table. What was wrong with the ad? There were no paper tags from the tea bags showing around the rim of the teapot. In a tea drinking country like India, the lower classes drink loose tea, while only the upper classes can afford to buy the more expensive tea bags. Again, the marketer's self-reference criterion got in the way of seeing this important difference.

Technology

The level of technological advancement in a country and the rate of technological change will influence the types of products that will be accepted and the means by which they should be introduced. Generally, countries that are highly advanced technologically are faster to accept innovations, and may in fact seek the latest "state of the art" products. However, cultural differences may underlie even such innocent-sounding assumptions as these. Take the case of West Germany, which by all accounts would be considered a technologically advanced market, eager to adopt the latest in high technology products. Yet as the head of Apple Computer's German operations observed, "If you don't take into account psychological factors, you make mistakes. You can't take California and transplant it to Germany."[5] West Germans have been slow (in U.S. terms) to adopt such high technology products as microwave ovens, cable TV, and cordless phones. The Germans even have a word to describe their reluctance to adopt new technology: *technologiefeindlichkeit*. It is estimated that only 5 percent of German white-collar workers use computers, and a recent survey showed that Germans believe computers make everyday life more difficult, restrict character development, and cause loneliness. Compare that to the U.S., Japanese, or Korean beliefs about computers and other high-tech gadgetry!

Some countries in the world have a suspicion of new and different products and a lack of understanding of technology. In such a case an existing product, redesigned in a simplified version, may be required to satisfy these markets. The old treadle and hand-operated Singer sewing machines are extremely popular in many LDCs, as are wringer washing machines; in the United States they are "antiques." A "classic" 1952 Cadillac in the United States is "just a car" in Egypt. Yet again, a word of warning to the wise is in order. Avoid making the same mistakes as some American manufacturers in thinking that yesterday's U.S. products will be acceptable to today's less developed countries. Widespread travel and communication have made these markets aware of the latest developments. Though a less advanced technology may be more suitable and less expensive in the eyes of the U.S. marketer, the LDC buyer may be insulted by such patronizing and may demand "the state of the art" (even if that is not truly what is meant).

Considering the cultural environment as a precipitating factor to discretionary change (as opposed to mandatory change) is not to diminish its importance. On the contrary, the cultural environment is the single most pervasive factor. Culture determines how and what people consume. A society's needs and wants, and the means of satisfying those needs and wants, are culturally determined. One of the most difficult barriers for an international marketer to cross is the cultural barrier. To do so the marketer must eliminate the SRC, or self-reference criterion, and instead begin to think in terms of the host country culture.

EXERCISE 2–1

Interview a foreign student who has only recently come to school in the United States. Focus your interview on the following topics by preparing a list of specific questions for each topic.

Favorite foods	National and local holidays
Family life	Education
National and local government	Religion
National heroes	Folklore

a. When you have completed the interview, ask yourself the same questions and draw a comparison between the two cultures.
b. Study the comparison and see if you can determine ways your SRC could influence your judgment about the student's culture.

POLITICAL AND GOVERNMENTAL FACTORS

The home country controls the movement of goods, services, and currency across its borders; therefore permission must first be obtained from the home government (in our case, the United States federal government) to do business internationally. The likelihood of obtaining that permission depends on the philosophy of the political forces in power at the time. Where political forces in the United States are often reluctant to back policies that directly affect the domestic economy, they are much less reluctant to tamper with international trade.

In much the same way, the government of the host country has the ultimate decision-making power regarding the activities of the multinational firm within its borders. Accordingly, the political and governmental environment of the host country under consideration should be researched as well. The following sections examine only some of the areas that require investigation; the point to keep in mind as you read is that the conduct of international business is accomplished only with the consent of the governments involved.

Type of Government

Knowing the type of government in the host country may, by definition, indicate something about the nature of business associations. In a republic or other parliamentary form of government, for example, the MNC (multinational corporation) is likely to be doing business with individuals, privately owned companies, or stockholder-owned corporations with little or no direct government intervention. In the United States and Canada, most corporations are either privately held (by individuals) or publicly owned (by shareholders); in either case, transactions are conducted freely between businesses, generally without interference from either country's government. Alternately, in Arab countries such as Saudi Arabia where the type of government is frequently a monarchy, businesses are most likely owned and operated by large families or clans. Here again, the foreign businessperson will negotiate business directly with the owners without government intervention. Such freedom from government intervention is not the situation surrounding the conduct of business in China or the Soviet Union. In countries such as these with a communist form of government, customers as well as business partners will frequently be government agencies or government-owned businesses.

In addition to influencing the nature of business associates, knowing the type of government can indicate the degree of government control and intervention that the MNC can expect. For example, in the Soviet Union the government owns and operates all businesses, setting goals for production based upon each successive Five Year Plan. Any foreign firm attempting to sell goods to the Soviet Union must therefore go through the appropriate ministry. If the good is specified as desirable for import under the Five Year Plan, the ministry may consent to negotiate with the foreign firm. Any and all business will be conducted with the government exclusively.

This is not to imply that multinational corporations should avoid doing business with Communist countries. In fact, the People's Republic of China has been quite aggressive in recent years in seeking U.S. business partners. The case of the state of Colorado provides an interesting example. The Hunan province in Central China, which is quite similar to Colorado in geography and resources, sought out the state of Colorado for a "sister state" relationship. Such an official relationship is designed to facilitate business relations between China and the United States (in this case, particularly between Hunan province and the state of Colorado). The Chinese provided a list of desired industries to the Colorado Lieutenant Governor, who then led a delegation from Colorado to visit Hunan province.

This initial, exploratory trade mission has been followed by a series of successive trade missions to China by Coloradans and by trade missions from China to Colorado. This is not an isolated case; in fact other states have similar sister-state arrangements with provinces throughout China. China's new attitude to enter world trade is a drastic change from earlier isolationist policies. The current political forces are committed to developing long-term business relationships with the West. As you can see from this example, it is not sufficient for the international marketer to know the current governmental situation; it will be necessary to be aware of imminent changes as well.

Instability and Political Risk

Even more important than knowing the type of government, the international marketer must be able to assess the stability of the political situation. In order to do any form of medium-term or long-term planning, which is prerequisite to entering international business negotiations, the firm must be assured of relatively stable government policies regarding foreign businesses. One of the more obvious examples of political instability was the revolution in Iran in 1974–75, when many foreign businesses that had thrived under the Shah were lost as the Ayatollah Khomeini came into power. Generally, however, the symptoms of political instability are a great deal more subtle than that. Two examples that illustrate the importance of carefully evaluating a country's degree of political risk follow.

Consider a country that most of you would say is relatively safe and secure: the United States. Certainly the United States is politically stable . . . or is it, where business is concerned? There is no question that we enjoy a democratic form of government that encourages free enterprise. We have a market economy open to international business. If consulted, you would assuredly recommend the United States as a safe bet—no riots, no military camps, no overthrow of governments in over 200 years. Yet, both U.S. and foreign international businesspeople are affected by changes in the federal government's trade policies. Imports into the United States are subject to the vagaries of government intervention, causing occasionally unstable business conditions.

On January 28, 1985, for example, President Reagan suddenly issued an emergency proclamation putting import quotas on certain categories of food. Why? Powerful lobbyists for the U.S. sugar industry had argued that businesses were sneaking into the United States food products made with sugar bought outside the United States at substantially lower world prices. These importers then extracted and sold the raw sugar in the United States for a substantial profit. Because the federal government restricts U.S. production to keep prices artificially high, U.S. sugar prices are nearly seven times that of world prices. In order to maintain the high prices, the United States must also restrict the importation of sugar, which it does by setting quotas. The emergency quota limit was reached on March 5, 1985, leaving U.S. importers of a variety of products in the lurch. For example, one food importer in Maryland lost 40 percent of his sales while marzipan, white chocolate, glazes, chocolate sauces, mousse mixes, and ice cream sprinkles (which he resells to hotels and restaurants) sat in warehouses waiting for clearance. The description of the goods listed in the quota was very broad and in addition to obviously sugar-laden products like those described above, a number of apparently unrelated products were also refused entry under the emergency quota. A New York bakery lost 20 percent of its business because it could not bring in the French and Italian pastries it resells. Another firm was unable to unload 20,000 Kosher pizzas it imported from Israel, and a New Jersey firm had to re-export its shipment of herb teas.[6] This situation was clearly not a very stable condition for the businesses involved, yet at first glance the United States does not appear to be a politically risky alternative.

Now let us look at another current global situation which, superficially at least, appears to present great political risk. In 1997 the People's Republic of China will be taking over control of Hong Kong. Parts of the area known as Hong Kong have been under a 99-year lease to the British—a lease that expires in 1997. Now it is well known that the British and the Chinese differ radically in their political and economic philosophies. Great Britain has a parliamentary form of government under a constitutional monarchy, and businesses generally enjoy a capitalist, free-market economy. At the other end of the spectrum, the Chinese Communist Party has ruled China since 1949, and the economy is planned under a series of Five Year Plans similar to the Soviet system. Yet the People's Republic of China recognizes that Hong Kong has flourished under capitalism and has signed a 50-year agreement to make no changes in the operation of Hong Kong, with the exception of military defense (the People's Army will move into Hong Kong). Most analysts believe that the situation, with respect to world trade, will remain quite stable.

As you can see from these two examples, simply knowing the type of government in a country may reveal the nature of business associations, but it will not provide the necessary insight to assess political risk. To do so, the firm must determine the philosophies of the various political parties, in and out of power, and estimate the degree and rate of possible political change.

Political Parties

As we discussed above, understanding the policies and the power bases of the political parties in the host country is essential. Even within the same country, with a single form of government, the host country may have a two-party or multiparty political system. It is likely that these political parties will have very different policies regarding international business. To illustrate, England has what could be considered a stable government, yet the leading political parties (Conservative and Labor) have opposing views of world trade. In a recent election, the conservative incumbent candidate (Margaret Thatcher) prevailed, and business continued as usual. However, had the Labor candidate won, foreign businesses would likely have seen more protectionist policies limiting the degree of their involvement in the United Kingdom.

The Effects of the U.S. National Image

A final political factor requiring investigation is the host country's attitude about the foreign business's home country. The U.S. MNC for example, is not just a "chemical company" or a "computer firm"; it is also perceived on a global basis as a representative of the United States. As such, it will be subjected to both the positive and the negative implications of carrying that image. Some countries and customers are pro-American, and demand is high for almost any product that is "made in America." However, some areas of the world are hostile to the U.S. government and its military or foreign policies, and vent their anger on American business. The rash of terrorism that plagued U.S. citizens and businesses abroad during the mid-1980s is a dramatic example.

LEGAL FACTORS

Multinational corporations must operate not only within the laws of the home country, but within the laws of the host countries as well. Legal restrictions can present absolute barriers to entry into a country, or can impose mandatory changes in product components, labeling, packaging, pricing, advertising, promotion, and even distribution. For example, advertisers in Europe must be extremely careful to design commercials that comply with all the laws within their viewing area. This is particularly difficult when satellites make transmissions possible across national boundaries, where not only specific laws differ but in fact entire legal systems may differ. When the European subsidiary of the General Mills toy group launched a campaign for Action Force war toys in Europe, they had to film two different commercials. The original version, for most of Europe, was done in a news program format, featuring the toy soldiers and tanks in war time. The second version, designed for Germany, Holland, and Belgium, replaces the toy tanks with jeeps and takes the guns out of the soldiers' hands (there is a strong political sentiment against armaments). But General Mills's problems were not over. In addition, France limited the amount of money the subsidiary could spend to advertise toys and games. The U.K. would not allow children to appear in ads and required that the toy autos in the commercials must follow adult road safety rules.[7]

As can be seen from these examples, complying with both home country and host country legal requirements can be extremely complex. As Newton Minow, attorney and former FCC chairman, commented on his study of the legal systems of four European countries, "In Germany, under the law everything is prohibited except that which is permitted. In France, under the law everything is permitted except that which is prohibited. In the Soviet Union, everything is prohibited, including that which is permitted. And in Italy, under the law everything is permitted, especially that which is prohibited."[8]

Code Law versus Common Law

Not only are there myriad laws on a variety of subjects throughout the world, but there are also a number of different legal systems. The U.S. legal system, as with most former British colonies, is derived from English common law. It is based on legal precedent and past practices and is interpreted by the courts. Other legal systems in the world are based on civil law or code law, which is an extensive system of specific rules and laws regulating commercial, civil, and criminal disputes. When firms from common law countries conduct business with code law countries it is essential that each tries to be as specific regarding meaning and intent as is possible. Misunderstandings regarding contract performance, rights of principals, legality of documents, and resolution of disputes can easily arise because of fundamental differences between the two systems.

Settling International Commercial Disputes

The bywords of international law are "conciliate; arbitrate; litigate"—
in that order. Litigation is quite costly not only in terms of money, but
in time, loss of confidentiality, and public relations problems. For these
reasons, companies prefer to settle disputes out of court and will generally agree upon third-party assistance in resolving their differences
well before any disputes arise. These agreements are formalized in
"arbitration clauses" of contracts and other legal documents and are
generally handled in the following manner.

Arbitration.   First, both parties must agree to arbitrate, if disputes
arise, by the rules of some stated arbitration tribunal. A number of
international arbitration groups have been organized for just that purpose, including the Inter-American Commercial Arbitration Association, the London Court of Arbitration, the American Arbitration
Association, and the International Chamber of Commerce. Second, both
parties must agree to abide by the decision of this board. If necessary,
most countries (including the United States) are prepared to legally
enforce performance of the terms of an arbitration clause entered into
by one of their citizens, corporate or individual.

If a dispute arises, the parties submit an application to the previously agreed upon arbitration board. The operations of the International Chamber of Commerce will provide a good example of typical
procedures. The ICC first attempts conciliation. If that fails, the arbitration process begins. Each party chooses an arbitrator from an ICC
list that include judges, lawyers, and other professionals; the ICC chooses
the third. The arbitrators hear both parties present their respective
cases and come to a decision, sometimes making an award. In international business this can be a particularly satisfactory way of resolving differences. Of more than 200 ICC cases, only 20 have been rejected
by the litigants. Of these, only one was reversed after further litigation.

Jurisdiction.   In the unlikely case that a dispute arises between
multinational companies (or between a government and an MNC) which,
for whatever reason, cannot be resolved through arbitration, the question becomes "where do we resolve the problem?" Disputes between
countries can be settled by the World Court at The Hague or the International Court of Justice of the United Nations, but no international
commercial court exists. Business disputes must be solved in the courts
of the home country of one of the participants or in the country where
the contract is performed. The decision as to which country's laws will
apply is best decided before any dispute arises. This may be accom-

plished by adding a jurisdiction clause to the contract, which states the mutually acceptable country of jurisdiction.

Intellectual Property Rights

A major international legal issue in recent years has been the protection of brand names, trademarks, patents, and other intellectual property rights. Companies who have licensed the use of their trademarks, brand names, or patents may be disappointed to find that royalty payments soon cease after the intellectual property rights are pirated by foreign firms. Counterfeiting is another serious problem, particularly for such globally well-known products as Cartier and Rolex timepieces. It is estimated that these companies have lost sales of more than 10 million watches and $500 million to counterfeiters. Hong Kong is considered to be a "world center" for counterfeit luxury consumer goods (Hermes scarves, Gucci bags), while Taiwan is the main source of counterfeit auto parts and batteries.

Not all intellectual property rights disputes are so dramatic. As we noted in the previous section, fundamental differences between common law and code law procedures can create problems. For example, prior registration of trademarks and brand names is necessary for ownership in code law countries, while prior use and tradition are the deciding factors in common law countries. Knowing this, a number of years ago one enterprising American residing in Mexico registered some 40 famous brand names and trademarks including Bromo Seltzer and Carter's Little Liver Pills. Since Mexico is a code-law country, this "entrepreneur" could legally register use of the tradenames, as he was the first to do so. He then collected substantial fees from firms forced to buy back the trademark or brand name. Lengthy litigation and help from the U.S. government was required to convince this enterprising gentleman to discontinue his operation.

ECONOMIC FACTORS

Why are the United States and Europe better potential markets for most companies than China or India? Certainly China's population of one billion or India's of over 750 million far surpass the U.S. population of 236 million or Europe's population of 490 million. The answer is well known to marketers: markets are more than just numbers of people. Markets are people with the willingness and ability to spend. Thus the high levels of discretionary income available to U.S. and European consumers, combined with their certainly adequate numbers, result in a market with greater potential than their Chinese or Indian counterparts, which have great numbers but little or no discretionary income. Yet, they too can be good markets for food, industrial products, and other goods and services that they need but do not produce.

Overall Level of the Economy

In order to estimate potential market demand, the economic environment must be researched. As a general indicator, the United Nations had devised a general classification system with which you may be familiar. MDCs, or more developed countries, include such nations as the United States, Canada, Germany, France, Sweden, Japan, and England. These countries are industrialized, have high per capita incomes, and are generally involved in world affairs. The LDCs, or less developed countries, include most of Asia, Latin America, and Africa. These nations are still developing industrially, are newly entering world trade, and have comparatively low per capita incomes. Two additional categories have recently been added to improve the classification system. LLDCs, or least developed countries, are the underdeveloped countries of the world; they are largely agrarian, subsistence societies with rural populations, extremely low per capita income levels, and little global involvement. Central Africa and parts of Latin America and Asia have LLDC nations, including Chad, Ethiopia, Bolivia, Pakistan, and Laos. In addition, several developing countries or LDCs have experienced relatively rapid industrial growth during the last few decades. They have grown more rapidly than many other LDCs and have had improvements in their general economic well-being. NICs, newly industrialized countries as they are sometimes called, do not fit the traditional pattern of economic development. NICs are characterized by high per capita incomes and rapid industrialization of targeted industries. South Korea, Singapore, Hong Kong, Mexico, Brazil, and Taiwan have become formidable rivals for MDCs in world markets for many products, including steel, shipbuilding, machine tools, and electronics. To cite one example, color televisions manufactured in Korea and Taiwan account for over 15 percent of the U.S. color television market.

Economic Change

As we can see by the example of the NICs, knowledge of the rate of change in the economy as well as the direction of change is necessary for market planning. After World War II Japan was a country devastated by the effects of war. Barely 40 years later, Japan is a leader in manufacturing and banking worldwide. Japanese consumer electronics firms such as Sony, Sanyo, and Mitsubishi dominate retail shelves; Japanese automobiles such as Honda, Nissan, Toyota, and Subaru outsell domestic automobiles in many markets (Subaru is the Number One selling car in Colorado). The Japanese stimulated the stagnant U.S. motorcycle market with their innovative and exciting new models, building markets where others thought none existed. One source calls Japan "the U.S. nemesis in world trade," for taking over such formerly U.S.-dominated markets as Saudi Arabia. Within a lifetime, U.S. managers are learning "the art of Japanese management," instead of vice versa.

Even more dramatic has been the rise of the NICs such as Taiwan and Korea. As few as 10 years ago the evaluation of the market potential of the NICs would have been entirely different than today: Not only have the NICs become greatly improved markets, but their rapid industrialization has made them formidable competitors. South Korea today is called the Second Japan, becoming a world-class industrial power in automobiles, steel, and semiconductors. The new Hyundai subcompact introduced to U.S. markets in 1986 is a source of national pride; Leading Edge is an "IBM-clone" microcomputer viewed as a tough competitor to Compaq and IBM. The Koreans have gained significant U.S. market share in microwave ovens, videotape recorders, and other markets. Taiwan has developed even more rapidly, with a per capita GNP of about $3,000—50 percent higher than South Korea's.

U.S. marketers can be certain that the next 10 years will bring even more drastic changes as China and many Third World nations aggressively enter world markets. When economically developing nations enter world trade, they bring with them special requirements. These LDCs see world trade as a means to improve domestic economic conditions and will seek products and business arrangements that provide capital and employment for their people. China, for example, expects foreign partners to provide money and expertise while China provides human resources. Mexico provides special "in-bond" areas for U.S. manufacturers who build factories in Mexico and employ Mexican workers to make consumer goods such as clothing and small household appliances (for export only). Many LDCs will make similar demands, seeking factories and production facilities, but discouraging or prohibiting the import of consumer goods. Many MNCs comply with these demands, in the long-term expectations that improved LDC economies will eventually lead to prospective consumers. Because of early LDC involvement by Gillette, Carnation, Nestle, and other MNCs, consumers in these developing countries will already be aware of these products when they have sufficient income to buy.

Evaluating Economic Data.   In the previous section, which discussed the overall economic levels of various countries, we compared levels of per capita income. This statistic is frequently used to estimate the general economic condition of a country, largely because it is a readily available and easily computed figure. However, a marketer must be able to look at the reality beyond the numbers. First, per capita income is an average figure; it gives no indication of income distribution. For example, many countries have a few very wealthy people and large numbers of poor people. Oil-rich Middle Eastern nations exemplify this pattern, with a few extremely wealthy families living in the same country with subsistence-level nomads. One company made an error of this type in estimating market potential for aerosol-spray furniture polish. Analysis of local average income levels suggested that the general population could afford the product. In reality, income averages were distorted by the great wealth of a very few. Those few who could afford the product saw no need for such labor-saving products for their servants.

Though per capita income is a readily available statistic for most countries, it is not the same as nor is it as useful as knowing household income. In many countries, especially in LDCs, the extended family is the norm, which indicates that there may be multiple wage earners per household. For example, in most Latin American countries, like Colombia or Venezuela, family households often include the nuclear family plus grandparents, aunts, uncles, cousins, and other family members. Two or three of the male family members may be wage earners for the group. Therefore, to understand relevant family buying behavior, the marketer must consider both the number of wage earners per household and the size of the household. Marketers must look at household income for MDCs in the same way. In the United States, for example, the typical household size is the nuclear family. In the 1950s that would have indicated one wage earner, but in the 1980s the nuclear family with one wage earner represented only 7 percent of all U.S. households. Today, most U.S. nuclear families' household incomes must include the wages of both husbands and wives.

In addition, per capita income only considers the legitimate money economy. Especially in less developed countries, a large part of the population may not be in "the economy" per se: They may be living a subsistence existence or supporting themselves through barter, the black market, and other means. Care must be taken when evaluating economic data to get a true picture of the local economy. This usually requires an understanding of more than just "the numbers." In fact, in some countries the "informal sector" may be larger than the "formal economy." Peru's official statistics report that more than half the population is living in poverty. Yet the Institute for Liberty and Democracy, a Peruvian group that has spent two years studying unregistered business, recently reported that every two out of three jobs, or 60 percent of the Peruvian economy, may be underground commerce. Peru's quagmire of business regulations has created what may be the world's largest black market: businesses that do not pay taxes or show up in official statistics. Millions of residents live in "informal" houses built by "informal" contractors with "informal" materials. Ninety percent of the clothing industry in Peru may be black market, with the workers riding to work in black market buses.

Peru is not a unique case. In the United States anywhere from 5 percent to 25 percent of the economy may be off-the-books; among the European Community, Italy has the largest black market. The Japanese Yakuza, or Mafia, controls a sizable portion of Japan's black market activity. Burma supplements its planned economy with an extensive black market economy. (Tourist guides claim that Johnny Walker Red Label scotch and American cigarettes bring the highest black market profits, at a 3-to-1 price increase.) A recent U.S. embassy report estimated that the "shadow economy" accounts for 80 percent of Burma's retail sales.

These examples highlight some of the problems facing the international marketer in using official statistics reported by the host country to such agencies as the IMF (International Monetary Fund), the UN (United Nations), or the World Bank. Though secondary data such as this are readily available, the sophisticated marketer must view all such reports with a skeptical eye and look beyond the official story. The careful interpretation and analysis of economic data is more critical than the mere accumulation of "facts."

Other Economic Conditions.   A number of additional factors must be considered before evaluation of a country's economic environment is complete. Business cycles (prosperity, decline, recession/depression, and recovery) affect both business behavior and consumer behavior. Because of the economic interrelationships and interdependencies created by international trade, business cycles often occur on a global level. For example, the U.S. Great Depression of the late 1920s and the early 1930s sent much of the world economy into a depression as well. In the 1980s, the severe recession of the U.S. economy and its subsequent recovery has been felt throughout the world. The European Community, in particular, as the major U.S. trading partner, tends to lag behind U.S. business cycles by about 18 months to two years. When the U.S. economy began to slide into a recession in the early 1980s, Europe was still producing goods for U.S. markets. U.S. consumers stopped buying, however, as expectations for the economy worsened. This reduction in U.S. buying dampened economic conditions in Europe, as export-related production fell off and workers were laid off. Europe followed the United States into recession. In 1984, the United States entered a cycle of economic recovery. Consumers in the United

States, once again optimistic about conditions, began buying German automobiles, French wines, and Italian leather shoes. This began to slowly stimulate European economies as inventories were depleted and production resumed. A positive economic situation for Europe, this U.S. shopping spree worsened the U.S. balance of trade deficit with Europe. Since U.S. recovery preceded the European recovery by about 18 months, the United States was buying from Europe, but Europe was not yet buying again from the United States. As you can see from this scenario, the economic interrelationships from world trade are quite complex, but are of critical importance to the international marketer attempting to predict international market demand.

A second critical economic factor, inflation, increases prices, reducing consumer demand for products and eating away at company profits. Some countries, including Israel, Brazil, and Argentina, have been fighting triple-digit inflation throughout the past decade. Argentina's inflation has been so severe that in 1986 the government replaced the Argentinian peso with the Austral in a drastic move to control inflation. (It took one million old pesos to get one Austral). Other moves include wage and price controls, which obviously affect international marketers. For example, drug companies such as Pfizer have been unable to increase their prices on over-the-counter drugs, yet face increasing costs of production and distribution. Eventually, they may be forced to pull out of certain markets.

Unemployment affects levels of consumer spending and foreign investment. Take the case of the European Community (EC), whose plan of increased coordination has had an unintended impact on labor conditions. The EC now has a European Community passport, is working on a European stamp, issues Eurodollars, and in general is working to facilitate the free flow of labor, goods, and capital between countries. As a result, however, MNCs use the free flow of labor as a bargaining tool in negotiating with labor. If unions in one country will not grant wage and benefit concessions to the company, the company will simply threaten to move the plant elsewhere. Workers in Hyster Co.'s Irvine, Scotland, forklift plant found this out the hard way when workers took a 14 percent pay cut, and managers an 18 percent pay cut, to keep a $60 million project in Scotland and out of Holland. Such actions have a twofold effect. In terms of consumer spending, some countries gain employment at the cost of reduced wage levels; their laborers are still in the consumer market yet at lower discretionary income levels. Other consumers, however, may benefit from the lower prices of goods, achieved through lower costs of production. In terms of foreign investment, those countries able to offer the lowest labor costs may be able to attract new foreign investment, or induce the relocation of current production facilities, thereby improving the local economy.

Just as in the domestic environment, then, economic conditions will uncontrollably affect business. As you can see from the previous discussion, business cycles, inflation, and unemployment affect the focus of supply and demand internationally in a manner often more complex than domestically.

MANDATORY TRADE BARRIERS

Important issues for a marketer to understand are the mandatory trade-related conditions for market entry. To that end, the political, legal, and economic environment of the host country will provide information regarding any potential trade barriers to doing business in the host country. These trade barriers may completely prevent trade in the prospective country, may discourage or place restrictions on trade, or may in fact promote trade. Understand that these conditions can and do change, but that trade conditions motivated by political or economic forces and enforced by legal or governmental decree are mandatory in nature and must be obeyed by the international marketer.

Barriers Prohibiting Foreign Trade and Investment

The most severe restrictions prohibit trade altogether. Trade barriers of this nature can originate from two sources, political and/or economic. In the first, political, one country prohibits trade with any firm from another country. For example, because of the Palestinian dispute, Arab countries do not trade with Israel, nor Israel with any Arab countries. The United States will not trade with any country that boycotts Israel. Yet political disagreements between nations are not the only sources of trade restrictions. The United States closely monitors the export of certain high technology products including computers and medical instruments. To discourage technology thieves, President Reagan signed a directive giving the Defense Department authority to review export licenses for Austria, Sweden, Switzerland, and other countries where U.S. products have been rerouted to unfriendly hands.

The second reason that trade may be prohibited is largely economic in nature. To protect their infant industries, NICs often prohibit imports of any goods that are domestically produced.

In addition, firms engaged in business relating to national defense (such as communications, transportation, or energy) or national resources (such as mining or agriculture) may be barred from foreign ownership. The most drastic examples of government intervention with foreign investment in these industries have been instances of expropriation, confiscation, nationalization, or domestication. Expropriation is the complete takeover of the foreign investment by the host country government with some amount of reimbursement. In 1938, for example, Mexico expropriated all foreign oil operations. With confiscation, the host country takes over foreign investment without reimbursement. In either case, if the host government then manages the confiscated or expropriated MNC, the company is said to be nationalized. Nationalization is often done on an industrywide basis; with the election of France's socialist leader in the 1980s, Francois Mitterand, many French industries were nationalized. If the host country coerces the MNC into selling controlling equity to nationals, the company is then said to have been domesticated.

These actions are taken by host governments to regain control of crucial industries that have become completely or predominantly foreign-owned. The industries most often expropriated or confiscated are those considered essential to national defense and national wealth. For example, the World Bank reports that since 1960, 1,535 firms from 22 different nations were expropriated in 511 separate actions by 76 nations! Between 1960 and 1974, 12 percent of all U.S. properties and 18 percent of all U.S. mining companies were expropriated. Latin America countries were responsible for 49 percent of the expropriations of U.S. investments, Arab nations for 27 percent, African nations for 13 percent, and Asian countries for 11 percent.

Other examples of government intervention in foreign business investment are not so dramatic, but still affect the nature and extent of foreign business. The next few sections will provide additional examples of government intervention in the conduct of international business, motivated by political or economic forces.

Restrictions Affecting Movement of Goods

Restrictions affecting imports can be classified into two basic categories: tariffs and nontariff barriers. Tariffs are taxes levied on goods as they enter the country, designed both to generate revenue and to discourage imports. The resulting increase in the price of the product may render it unmarketable or unprofitable from the point of view of the firm. From the viewpoint of the consumer, tariffs increase prices and reduce product choices.

In one approach to combating these trade barriers, the United States, with 22 other countries, signed the General Agreement on Tariffs and Trade (GATT). GATT now counts 85 countries in its membership. Since its inception in 1947, GATT has worked successfully to reduce tariffs worldwide. For example, at the height of protectionism in the 1932 depression era, average tariff levels in the MDCs reached 50 to 60 percent. Today tariffs average 8.3 percent in the United States, 9.8 percent in the European Community, 10.9 percent in Japan, and

15.5 percent in Canada; these will be further reduced by 1988. The 1979 Tokyo Round (GATT's intergovernmental meetings are called rounds) was the first to address nontariff barriers such as quotas, standards, subsidies, and documentation.

Nontariff barriers are serious impediments to trade which have increased with worldwide recession and reductions in tariffs. Quotas limit the quantity of goods that can enter a country; for example, Japanese quotas on citrus fruits and melons have effectively raised the price of a honeydew melon to $35.00 in Tokyo. The United States recently asked Japan to place a "voluntary" quota on automobile exports, reducing the number of Japanese cars shipped to the United States. Quotas are not something only other countries do. The United States imposes quotas too. There are quotas on sugar, as discussed earlier, and a variety of products including textiles, steel, and shoes. Standards are a more insidious trade barrier. These are extraordinarily stringent product requirements affecting packaging, labeling, testing methods, quality standards, and other areas that can make it virtually impossible for a product to enter the country. Documentation (i.e., bureaucratic red tape) may also discourage imports in a similar manner, by requiring that a great many meticulously completed documents involving many parties accompany product shipments.

Restrictions Affecting Movement of Currency

Governments not only control the movement of goods across borders, but also control the transfer of money across international borders. These interventions by governments may take a variety of forms, depending on the political or economic objectives. Exchange controls may be instituted for economic reasons, such as when a country faces a shortage of foreign exchange. In such times, currencies may be blocked; that is, prevented from leaving the country. Recently the Philippines halted all movement of U.S. dollars. This posed a problem for companies doing business there. Since dollars were prohibited from leaving the Philippines, there was no money to buy goods from abroad and profits could not be sent to the parent company. In short, any activity that required currency to be spent outside the Philippines was curtailed. If currency blocks last for an extended period, companies may have to cease operations.

In other countries, such as Mexico, Argentina, and other LDCs, fixed exchange rates will vary depending on the reason for wanting the exchange. When exchange rates are controlled by a country, an exchange permit, requesting an amount of foreign currency, is obtained from the country's central bank. Currency needed to purchase foreign luxuries often carries high exchange rates, while necessities get favorable rates. For example, luxuries may receive a 20 to 1 exchange rate, that is, it takes 20 units of the local currency to buy 1 unit of the foreign currency. Necessities, on the other hand, may receive a five to one rate, that is, five local currency units for one foreign currency unit. That is why foreign students often receive favorable rates of exchange from their home countries while vacationers traveling abroad receive unfavorable rates. Exchange risk can also be a serious problem when the country's balance of payments is unfavorable or unstable, because the country will not want precious capital to leave its borders. For these reasons, members of the Andean common market (ANCOM includes Colombia, Peru, Bolivia, Ecuador, and Venezuela) require that foreign investors repatriate (send home) no more than 20 percent of the direct capital that they invest. In any case, currency convertibility risk can pose serious problems for the international firm, since taking money (i.e., profits) out of the country is at the whim of the host nation and may change unpredictably. More on the problems of exchange risk will be covered in the chapter on pricing.

Restrictions Affecting Business Structure and Operations

Restrictions of this type—which affect the business structure or operations of the MNC in the host country—can also take a variety of forms, depending upon the purpose they were designed to serve. The following examples demonstrate a few of the ways in which governments have controlled foreign business investment and their reasons for doing so.

Governments frequently restrict the industries that foreign investors can enter. ANCOM, for example, allows no new foreign investment in extractive, public utility, publishing, communications, or banking industries. As we discussed previously, industries that are vital to national defense or involve natural resources are usually off-limits.

Business structure may also be controlled. For example, the People's Republic of China (PRC) recently opened its doors to foreign investment to joint equity ventures. The foreign partners must provide at least 25 percent of the capital with no upper limits. Contributions of capital from the foreign party may take the form of cash, machinery, or technology. China provides human resources, sites for factories, and other local resources. The company will be managed by a five-member board of directors with appointees from both sides and a Chinese chairman.

Countries may try to control company operations. The Mexican Ministry of Commerce and Industrial Development recently announced that by 1987 each foreign automobile maker would be restricted to building one type of car, and not more than five models of that type.

Twenty-five percent of the cars should be inexpensive, stripped-down models; and auto makers should plan on increasing the use of locally made parts and materials. This move made changes in the operations of the six major foreign automobile manufacturers, including General Motors Corp., Ford Motor Company, Chrysler Corp., Volkswagenwerk-AG, Nissan Motor Company, and Regie Nationale des Unines Renault (working with its 46 percent–owned U.S. affiliate American Motors Corp.).

Finally, the firm should examine the host country's attitude regarding multinational business investment. To illustrate with an example from Canada, of the 100 largest Canadian firms, 37 are U.S.-owned or controlled. U.S. companies own 39 percent of Canada's manufacturing industries, 32 percent of the pulp and paper industry, and 36 percent of the mining and smelting industries. Not surprisingly, Canada has taken steps to limit and control foreign investment. Canada requires foreign investors to: (1) sell a sizable minority of equity to Canadian nationals; (2) appoint Canadians to the board of directors and to key managerial positions; (3) purchase supplies and materials from Canadian companies; and (4) concentrate marketing efforts on export markets.

LDCs often demand community involvement on the part of the MNC. H. J. Heinz Company was permitted to purchase 51 percent of Zimbabwe's largest producer of cooking oil, Olivine Industries, only after Heinz's president convinced the Zimbabwe Prime Minister that Heinz would provide agricultural expertise and help develop local farmers. Such agricultural development provides Heinz with a source of agricultural raw materials for many of its products and improves the living standards of this Third World country. In turn, an improved economy means more potential Heinz consumers.

Coca-Cola has also been involved in goodwill projects around the world, since as a nonessential industry Coke must always be aware of its "guest" status. Coca-Cola planted thousands of acres of orange trees in Cairo; built a tomato paste factory in Turkey; and helped construct a whey protein plant in the Soviet Union. Such actions by companies like H. J. Heinz, Coca-Cola, and others including Nestle, Carnation, and CPC International are evidence of long-term planning on the part of MNCs to penetrate the developing Third World markets. LDCs who are struggling to develop their economies are likely to demand such concessions as these from MNCs to further their plans for economic development.

SUMMARY

As you can see, the study of the foreign uncontrollable elements is varied and complex. A thorough understanding of all relevant uncontrollable elements, their interaction, and their impact on marketing is crucial. Research regarding political, legal, or economic factors will reveal possible barriers to trade or mandatory changes that must be made in the marketing plan. Knowledge of the many cultural influences will guide the marketer to the kinds of discretionary changes that might facilitate effort to overcome market barriers. In the next chapter we will look at some of the problems facing a marketer about to conduct marketing research.

NOTES

1. John S. Hill and Richard R. Still, "Adapting Products to LDC Tastes," *Harvard Business Review,* March–April 1984, p. 95.
2. Lennie Copeland and L. Griggs, *Going International* (New York: Random House, 1985), p. 48.
3. Vern Terpstra, *The Cultural Environment of International Business* (Cincinnati: South-Western Publishing, 1985), pp. 45–48.
4. David A. Ricks, *Big Business Blunders* (Homewood, Ill.: Dow Jones-Irwin, 1983), p. 66.
5. Peter Gumbel, "Germans and Computers: Do They Mix?" *The Wall Street Journal,* April 17, 1986, p. 30.
6. "Why Israeli Pizzas and Korean Noodles Find Door Slammed," *The Wall Street Journal,* April 23, 1985, p. 1.
7. "Global Ads for Kids Stymie Parker Bros.," *Advertising Age,* June 25, 1984, p. 72.
8. "On the Record," *Time,* March 18, 1985, p. 73.

ADDITIONAL READINGS

Cateora, Philip. *International Marketing.* 6th. ed. Homewood, Ill.: Richard D. Irwin, 1987, chs. 4–8.

Fields, George. *From Bonsai to Levi's.* New York: Macmillan, 1983.

Goans, Judy W. "A Guide to Protecting Intellectual Property Rights." *Business America,* October 27, 1986, pp. 2–7.

Terpstra, Vern. *The Cultural Environment of International Business.* Cincinnati: South-Western Publishing, 1985.

CHAPTER THREE

International Marketing Research

One critical prerequisite for successful marketing is good information. The marketing concept clearly implies that the old attitude "just add shipping costs to the product and send it overseas" is destined to fail in today's competitive international markets. Understanding consumer needs and understanding how best to satisfy those needs are incumbent upon the international marketing executive. Even in domestic markets, current, accurate information is needed to perform that function; to achieve success in international markets, the firm's information needs are magnified.

THE IMPORTANCE OF INTERNATIONAL MARKETING RESEARCH

Entering an international market can be a long-term and costly prospect; at a minimum it is certainly riskier than entering a domestic market. The amount of time and expense associated are tied directly to the firm's planned level of involvement and subsequently to the form of the firm's business structure. (To illustrate, exporting generally requires less capital investment and may be of shorter term than a joint venture.) As the firm becomes more committed to international markets, and as investments in time and capital increase, the need for information becomes more critical. From this perspective, let us first examine what international marketing research can do for the firm.

Good research can help prevent costly mistakes. One well-known multinational fiber producer planned to build a pulp processing plant in Italy. It purchased a large tract of land covered with eucalyptus trees with the thought to use the trees as the raw materials source. As a cost-cutting measure, the company decided against sending a tree specialist to Sicily. It was not until after the plant was built and production ready to begin that the firm discovered that the trees were too small, the supply too limited, and the logs unsuitable for use. The comparatively minor up-front cost of marketing research might have saved the firm from later suffering a $55 million loss.

Marketing research can help to ensure that the company's name will be well received. Because of the long-term nature of international marketing, it is important for the firm to establish and maintain a positive global image. In addition, successful initial product introduction is used as the groundwork for later adding more products to the line. When Binoca launched a marketing campaign for its talcum powder in India, its advertising showed a beautiful but apparently nude woman applying powder. The copy, strategically placed to cover parts of her body, read, "Don't go wild—just enough is all you need of Binoca talc." The conservative Indian public found the ads indecent and developed strong negative associations with the Binoca name.[1] This firm too learned the importance of marketing research only when it was too late.

Marketing research can help to identify opportunities as well as risks. After World War II, spare parts made specifically for use in Caterpillar Tractor equipment hit the market—parts neither approved nor manufactured by Caterpillar Tractor Company. Had the company been aware of the demand, it might have been first to develop a profitable market.[2]

Finally, decisions about business structure can be improved with marketing research. One U.S. pharmaceutical company discovered this when it licensed its manufacturing techniques to an Asian company, which heavily promoted the products with great success. The terms of the deal were such that the licensee (the Asian company) retained almost all of the profits. Because the U.S. company failed to research the market adequately they did not realize the enormous potential demand. If they had been aware of the market's possibilities, they might have entered a joint venture agreement more favorable to the firm.

Well-conceived and well-implemented marketing research can provide a company with the information to make sound strategic decisions. Identifying international market opportunities and risks, determining the nature of the business the firm should be in and the appropriate structure for that business, and developing tactical plans for successful market penetration are all improved with good marketing research.

PLANNING FOR INTERNATIONAL INFORMATION NEEDS

Considering the copious amounts of information required and its complex nature, it is necessary to bring some order to the international marketing research process. One general rule is to start with broad research areas and to gradually narrow the scope of the research (think of an inverted pyramid). *Strategic* decisions made at top corporate levels require general kinds of information. The country analysis is usually the first step, examining the foreign uncontrollable elements (discussed in Chapter 2) and general business conditions. If there are no major stops—no insurmountable barriers—then the information is analyzed to estimate market potential. With evidence of sufficient market potential, research then focuses on information for *tactical* decisions. These are largely the province of the marketing department and require specific, detailed information for evaluating the nature and extent of changes to the marketing mix (see Exhibit 3–1).

Step One: Country Analysis

This first step involves a broad overview of the country or region under consideration. The research centers on answering questions about the foreign uncontrollable elements as discussed in depth in the previous chapters. To review quickly, researchers will investigate *political* factors such as the significance of and frequency of elections; the political party system, including party policies and philosophies; the government's view of the United States and of U.S. MNCs; the stability and rate of change of the government; and the overall foreign investment climate. They will ask questions regarding the *economic* climate including the general economic level, its rate of change, key economic indicators, economic structure, and capital movement. The *legal* system, particularly with respect to commercial law, will be scrutinized for possible barriers to trade or other influences on the prospective business. Particularly important are the many *cultural* factors, such as language, aesthetics, education, social groups, science, technology, and religion. Examining the general conditions of the country should reveal any significant barriers to business. For example, evidence of boycotts, serious political instability, or cultural taboos against the product would prevent the firm from attempting to enter the market. Having reached this conclusion, marketing research would terminate at this point until the delimiting conditions changed. If no insurmountable barriers are encountered, the research continues.

For strategic decisions, the firm will also require information regarding *business operations* in the country. *Financial data* such as currency exchange rates and fluctuations, availability of capital, level of interest rates, and taxes should be collected. The firm will require *management and administrative data* including information regarding local labor practices, reporting procedures, and management skills; *operations data* concerning electrical systems, measurement systems,

EXHIBIT 3–1   Scope of International Marketing Information Needs (nature of information needs at various stages)

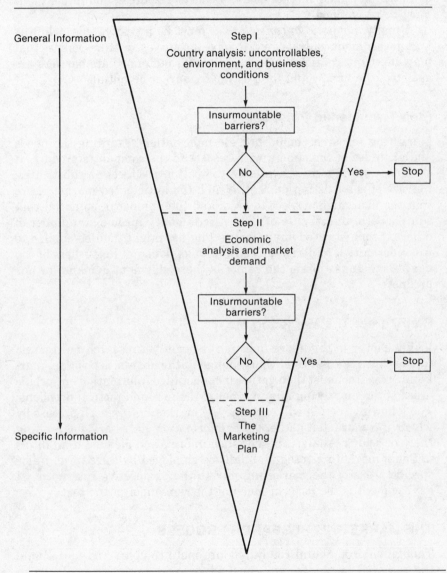

costs of energy, and level of infrastructure; and information regarding sources of raw material and supplies. In addition, the number and size of *competitors,* their market share, products, resources, and future plans must be researched.

Finally, *domestic uncontrollables* must be investigated, including U.S. government controls, restrictions, incentives, or other policies that may affect international business plans. If no immediate barriers are detected, the firm would then estimate market potential.

Step Two: Market Potential

Marketing research should provide information regarding the needs and attitudes of consumers with respect to the company's product. It should examine locally available competing products or substitutes; the size of the existing market, if any; the anticipated market share that the firm might expect to gain; and the number of potential consumers with an estimate of their discretionary income. A number of different sophisticated analytical techniques might then be applied to this information to derive an estimation of demand. Regardless of the method, the question is the same: Is there sufficient demand for our product?

Step Three: The Marketing Mix

If the answer to the above question is negative, research need go no further until market conditions change. If the answer is positive, marketing research must then gather more detailed information on specific areas of the marketing mix in order to make sound tactical decisions. The following section will examine the marketing research process by which the marketer gathers the information necessary for making these decisions. Analysis of how such information gleaned from international marketing research might be employed by the firm to tailor specific areas of the marketing mix to the prospective international environment is the focus of much of the remainder of the text.

THE MARKETING RESEARCH PROCESS

Though environmental conditions are more complex and varied and the research is broader in scope, the research process employed in international marketing is the same as the process utilized domestically. The research objectives are identical: to provide current, useful, and accurate data for marketing decisions. The procedure is the same: (1) define the problem; (2) gather data (you may be familiar with the terminology: "situation analysis," "informal investigation," and "formal investigation"); (3) analyze and interpret the data; and (4) report results. The major difference with international marketing research is the degree of difficulty with which the research is accomplished. This section will concentrate on steps 1 and 2, elaborating on some of the challenges posed in conducting international marketing research.

PROBLEM DEFINITION

The most important step in the marketing research process involves correctly defining the problem. In international marketing this is even more complex because of the self-reference criterion (SRC). It is very easy to look at a situation in the host country and to define it in home country terms. For example, a U.S. manufacturer of dishwashers introduced the product to Swiss markets using the same promotional appeal as in the United States—convenience. The firm did not research the effectiveness of the convenience appeal but assumed (incorrectly) that the Swiss consumers would respond as U.S. markets had. What the firm did not realize was that the Swiss housewife is involved in her role as homemaker. She rejected the idea of being replaced by a machine and, consequently, sales flopped. Later in-depth research revealed the real source of the problem, and the product was successfully repositioned as a hygiene product. Swiss housewives place great value on cleanliness, and they responded favorably to a "kills bacteria and germs" appeal.[3] Here, SRC caused the marketers to make decisions based on assumptions rather than well-researched facts.

Cultural differences in attitudes, norms, and values may also serve to distract the marketer from the real problem, especially if the SRC is not identified. For example, different values are placed on brand names or product type because of socioeconomic differences among countries. In Asia or Latin America an automobile is a luxury, but in the United States it is virtually considered an appliance. This difference in perception of value must be considered when marketing the product since pricing, promotional messages, product design, and even distribution will be affected. Levels of economic development will indicate differences in acceptable substitutes: In South America washing machines compete against servants as well as other brands of washing machines. Servants may be the ultimate user of the product, but the employer may define the servant's needs and be the decision maker for the purchase. Cultural differences will imply different conceptual perspectives, including (for example) something as seemingly universal as time. U.S. preoccupation with time-saving devices (instant soups, instant cereals, instant coffee, microwave ovens, etc.) is a mystery to much of the world, where they do not share our time-conscious values.

These examples are only a sample of the multitude of ways that subtle cultural differences can result in misidentification of a problem.

The international marketing researcher must be careful to state the problem in sufficiently broad terms. Because of the unfamiliar cultural environment, a broad problem scope will help to ensure that no significant factors are inadvertently omitted. The experience of a major U.S. cereal manufacturer provides a good example. The company researched the Japanese breakfast market and came to the conclusion that there was adequate potential demand to successfully introduce cold breakfast cereals. The Japanese were light breakfast eaters; the large numbers of working people would probably respond well to quick and convenient meal preparation; and the Japanese have large discretionary incomes. Sales, however, were dismal. The problem had been too narrowly defined, and the research never revealed the Japanese distaste for most dairy products, particularly milk.

INFORMATION GATHERING

As in domestic marketing research, the international information-gathering stage begins with secondary data collection. Because of the broad scope and consequently enormous information requirements of international marketing research, secondary data are particularly important in the early stages. Previously published data provide a relatively fast means of gaining some initial awareness of a country and providing a framework for further analysis. Specific areas of interest which are inadequately addressed are then pinpointed for further research, and the required primary data are collected to flesh out the report. When conducting international marketing research, data collection is often difficult, time-consuming, and expensive. This section will discuss sources of data and some of the advantages and disadvantages of both secondary and primary data.

Secondary Data: Advantages and Disadvantages

Secondary data are particularly important for developing an initial overview of the country and identifying those areas that merit in-depth research. At times, the information obtained via secondary research will be sufficient to detect the more serious barriers to market entry early enough in the research process to preclude the need for further study. In other situations, secondary data will be valuable in assessing potential global opportunities that may merit further primary research.

Unlike much of the world, American businesses are accustomed to having an abundance of high-quality secondary data at their disposal. Most major public libraries have extensive reference sections that make a wide variety of sources available at no cost. In addition, chambers of commerce, trade associations, and a number of government agencies collect and publish data useful to marketers. Besides being readily available and easy to obtain, information is frequently offered free of charge. Equally as important, U.S. data are both timely and relatively accurate. U.S. economic figures are published quarterly or annually, as are many trade association reports. A complete U.S. census is compiled each decade. Private research firms such as Dow Jones or Standard & Poor's publish economic figures throughout the year, and the U.S. Securities and Exchange Commission requires public companies to publish financial statements annually. Because U.S. secondary data are relatively easy and inexpensive to collect, and cover a wide variety of subjects in an accurate and timely manner, the marketing researcher starts the investigation here.

International researchers do not enjoy the same luxuries in secondary data as researchers in U.S. markets. First of all, the marketing researcher should always maintain a healthy skepticism about the accuracy of secondary data. Much of the data is self-reported, and countries may (for example) have an interest in exaggerating literacy rates, GNP, population figures, or economic conditions. Many times data are unavailable or hopelessly outdated. Oman, Qatar, and Laos have never taken a census; Bolivia's last census was in 1950. In addition, the manner in which data are reported may render the information useless. Germany classifies television sets under "recreation and entertainment" while the United States classifies the same item as "furniture, furnishings, and household equipment," making it virtually impossible to isolate and compare figures on television sets alone. Another disadvantage to secondary data is that it is macroeconomic in nature and often not specific enough to be useful to marketers. For example, we have discussed the potential distortion problems inherent in relying on aggregated figures such as per capita income levels or overall GNP. When this is the case, primary research may be required to fill in the information gaps and to gain specificity.

In general, as a country's level of economic development improves, the availability and accuracy of its recorded data improves as well. While international data sources have improved markedly in many countries over the past few decades, adequate secondary data remain a problem for international marketing research.

Secondary Data Sources

The U.S. Department of Commerce (DOC) is the foremost government agency involved in promoting the expansion of U.S. business in international trade. Information is available through personal consultations at any of the many field offices and through a plethora of published materials. The DOC publishes a weekly newsletter (*Business America*) on international business activity, quarterly reports on international economic indicators, and annual reports on U.S. participation in foreign markets (e.g., *Foreign Trade Reports* on exports and *Market Share Reports* on market share in manufacturing). In addition to the information available on imports/exports and global economic indicators, the DOC publishes country analyses (*Overseas Business Reports* or *OBRs*), trade lists (lists of distributors and agents), and information on international financing or insurance. The *International Marketing Handbook* provides an in-depth report on 138 countries. A computer matching service called *Trade Opportunities Program* (*TOP*) matches U.S. sellers with foreign buyers. The U.S. Department of Commerce information can be supplemented by publications of the Bureau of the Census, State Department, and Department of Agriculture.

Global agencies are another prolific and relatively reliable source of information. The United Nations publishes the *Statistical Yearbook* which provides detailed demographic, economic, political, cultural, and geographic information. The World Bank publishes comprehensive statistics on a number of indicators including demographics, production, demand, industrialization, trade, energy, literacy, health, life expectancy, and social and military spending. They also publish *Country Economic Reports* which are highly detailed studies of macroeconomic and industry-specific trends.

Regional agencies and foreign governments also publish information. The EC (European Community), COMECON (Council for Mutual Economic Assistance), and the OECD (Organization for Economic Cooperation and Development) all provide information about their members. Many foreign governments publish statistics, but language may be a problem with these sources. Australia, China, and Norway publish in English, but Swiss statistics are in French and German.

Trade organizations are good sources of information. Many countries have American Chambers of Commerce offices as well as local Chambers of Commerce. These offices often have research libraries available and are usually able to provide up-to-date insight on a region. Major corporations including Price Waterhouse and Chase Manhattan Bank publish information; American University publishes Area Handbooks for most countries. Private businesses such as Business International publish regional and country reports.

As you can see, the sources of secondary data are many and varied. With this as a starting point, the marketing researcher can develop a fairly detailed picture of the prospective country or region. Any specific gaps might then be filled in with primary data.

Primary Data: Uses and Applications

Secondary data are largely in the form of macroeconomic indicators or other quantitative countrywide generalizations, and as such they may not provide the level of specificity required by marketers. Consumer buying behavior, attitudes about products or promotional messages, relevance of product attributes, product positioning, and other manifestations of cultural and societal norms are usually product- or industry-specific and must be gathered by primary research. This information may be critical to sound tactical decisions and usually warrants the time, energy, creativity, and expense required to collect it.

As an example, the traditional buyer of household appliances in the United States was "the housewife." Companies directed advertising to that target market through women's magazines and via commercials on daytime television depicting "housewifely scenarios" and promoting the labor-saving attributes of the product. However, in many countries consumer buying behavior may differ. In some cultures the male may be the principal decision maker or, as mentioned earlier, the actual buyer and user may be a servant, and the purchase decision may be made by the employer. An appeal to a female could prove offensive to a male purchaser, and a time-saving message would have no appeal to an employer considering purchasing the product for servant use. However, a product that did the job "better" (cleaner, shinier, etc.) might convince the employer to buy. Such situations indicate the need for different approaches to promotional planning in some countries.

Attitudes about products may vary as well. In Mexico a refrigerator is a symbol of status among lower-middle-income families and is frequently placed in the living room. In Africa it is a symbol of white man's power and may be prominently positioned in the home, even though there is no electricity and the appliance does not operate. The Japanese do not like the noisy motors on most refrigerators, as the sound carries annoyingly through the thin panels that create walls in the Japanese home. Most Europeans as well as Japanese prefer a smaller model refrigerator than Americans. Besides being a better fit in their smaller homes, few other cultures store as much food as Americans, or choose to pay for the myriad "luxury" features such as instant ice water or built-in digital clocks. Information of this nature can often be gathered only through primary research.

Primary research can reveal consumer attitudes relevant for product positioning. In the United States, adult education is pursued for personal enrichment or social contact; in Japan it is intended to improve work performance and to make business connections. Proper product positioning and subsequent promotional, pricing, and distribution decisions may depend upon this type of information.

Similarly, product attributes can vary between cultures. In France, for example, the hot-cold continuum is important in characterizing consumers' perceptions of fragrance, while to consumers in the United States or the U.K. hot-cold is not associated with scents.[4] A marketing researcher in France would therefore require this information to accurately determine consumer intentions about the product. For example, if Revlon were testing a new perfume in France, the marketing department would want to measure consumer perceptions of hot-cold with regard to the new perfume vis-à-vis the other perfumes on the market. Again, product positioning, pricing, and promotional messages might be affected by this information. Primary research would be one way to reveal the importance of this product attribute.

Finally, information describing cultural and societal norms is important for tactical marketing mix decisions. One example of the sometimes surprising cultural differences in perceptions involves Guinness Stout. Considered a hearty "male" drink for the Irish and English, in Hong Kong Guinness is reported to be an excellent drink for pregnant or menstruating women.[5] Without this information an executive planning marketing strategy for Guinness Stout in Hong Kong might make quite an embarrassing (not to mention costly) error.

Primary Data: Procedures and Problems

As useful as primary data can be, you are probably aware that even in the United States it can be difficult, time-consuming, and expensive to collect. As we shall see with many aspects of international marketing, any problems typically encountered domestically are magnified and multiplied internationally. Marketing research is no exception. This section will briefly review some of the procedures involved in gathering primary data and will investigate some of the problems associated with international primary marketing research. Keep in mind, however, that the costs of attempting to devise or implement a marketing plan without the information gleaned from conducting primary research can be even more costly.

Research Techniques

In the section on problem definition we discussed some of the difficulties encountered in isolating the central issue for international marketing research. Only when the marketer has identified the specific areas for study, however, can the appropriate research technique be selected. In multicountry research the survey technique is most frequently used, though observational or projective techniques may also be employed. Regardless of the research techniques selected, problems arise in any number of areas. Some of the typical problem areas include instrument design, sampling, and survey administration.

Instrument Design.   Asking the right questions is always a problem, even in domestic marketing. Questions that elicit the information desired without "leading the witness" are difficult to construct and to administer. It is also difficult to design questions that get at the heart of the matter; the marketer may ask questions that seem to be relevant (according to the marketer's SRC), but which may not get at the issues most salient to the respondent. In cross-cultural surveys misunderstandings easily arise. In one case, a survey conducted in West Germany asked about the number of "washers" produced in a given year. The answer reflected the production of flat metal discs instead of washing machines, which was the information desired.

Translation problems exacerbate an already difficult problem. "Back translation" is used to reduce misunderstandings. To illustrate: a statement is translated from English to Spanish by one translator, then a second party translates from Spanish back into English. The two statements (the original English version and the "back-translated" English version) are then compared. This is done to catch any possible misunderstandings before it is too late. If General Motors had used this technique, they may have discovered that the slogan "Body by Fisher" was sometimes translated as "Corpse by Fisher," and Pepsi might have anticipated that their "Come Alive with Pepsi" campaign would be interpreted by some cultures as "Come out of the Grave with Pepsi"!

Double meanings create similar problems, which can be prevented to a certain degree by back-translation. Several major tobacco companies could have prevented confusion when their "low-tar" cigarettes were interpreted as "low-asphalt" cigarettes, to the bewilderment of the consumers.

Even with the same language, care must be taken when going from country to country. Parker Pen, (internationally known as Parker, Inc.) tested the use of the word "bola" to describe its ballpoint pen in several Latin countries. To some it means "ball," but to others it meant "revolution," a "lie," or "fabrication," and in one country it was an obscenity. A marketer conducting research for a clothing or textile firm in England had better be aware that a sweater is called a jumper or jersey; a blouse is called a tunic; sneakers are plimsoles; garters are called suspenders; and suspenders are called braces. The use of personal interviewers who can explain confusing terms may be necessary until the "bugs" are worked out.

Response Error.   Once the questions are designed, the researcher may still have difficulties getting responses. Business owners in other countries may be suspicious of people asking questions, fearing tax auditors. Though the SEC requires U.S. public companies to disclose operating figures, few other countries have such requirements, and businesses are unused to revealing operational information. Individuals may be reticent to answer questions as well. Many cultures are extremely reluctant to talk about personal matters with strangers. In addition, it may be impossible to interview the desired individual; although women in the Middle East may make or influence purchase decisions, an interviewer would probably be forbidden to speak with them. The interviewer may also misinterpret responses because some emotional or societal concepts are manifested differently in other cultures. Public kissing and embracing may be a "social nicety" in European cultures, yet is a sign of affection in the United States. Laughter can be an expression of amusement or joy, but in West African countries it indicates embarrassment, discomfort, or surprise. Questionnaire design and interviewer analysis must be careful to avoid confusion resulting from misinterpreting these differences.

Sampling Error.   Sampling may be difficult or impossible in many countries, particularly LDCs. For example, typical lists that are used as sampling frames in the United States are simply unavailable in some parts of the world. Neither Cairo nor Tehran, with populations of 8 million and 5 million respectively, have telephone books. Saudi Arabia has neither street names nor house numbers. Street maps are frequently unavailable in parts of South America, Mexico, or Asia. As a result, marketers conducting international research often rely upon nonrandom procedures such as convenience, cluster, or area sampling. Though unsuitable for inferential statistical analysis, these methods are usually more cost efficient and may in fact be the only viable alternative.

Survey Administration.   Data collection techniques also vary greatly throughout the world. Implementation in LDCs requires some particularly creative thinking on the part of marketers used to MDC markets. For example, LDCs generally have low literacy rates, making written surveys impractical for the general public. Mail surveys are rarely used, due to the low literacy rates and poor postal systems. In fact, mail surveys are impossible in countries such as Chile where the receiver is expected to pay one half of the postage. However, mail surveys may be applicable for industrial research, assuming the researcher can contact the relevant respondent. Low levels of telephone ownership in some countries often preclude the use of telephone surveys. In addition, even where telephones are available, lines may be very difficult to get and costs may be prohibitive. Again, telephones may have more effective application in industrial research, as most business will have a telephone.

All this points to the use of personal interviews. Generally a more expensive technique, personal interviews may be the only way to reach the desired target market. Personal interviewing allows the interviewer to probe for answers and to explain confusing or ambiguous terms. Care must be taken since this advantage also has a corresponding disadvantage. Interviewer bias and bias from interviewer-respondent interaction may distort results. In addition, the firm may encounter difficulty in finding competent interviewers conversant in the native language as well as the language of the researchers.

As you may have deduced by now, there is no clear formula for action. The marketing researcher must continually make decisions regarding instrument design, research design, formulation of questions, sampling, or choice of interviewers based on determination of the techniques most suitable for the culture and environment.

Test Marketing.   For products that have successfully passed through nearly all the stages of the product development process, test marketing is often the final hurdle before full commercialization. The ideal situation in a test market is for consumers to be unaware that their city is the site of a commercial experiment. For example, residents of San Diego, California, saw television commercials and billboards for Coors Light beer, found Coors Light on the shelves of liquor stores, and heard ads for Coors Light on the radio. They were blissfully unaware that they were among the very few in the country who were being exposed to the new product, or that they were being closely monitored for their responses over a three-month period. This helps create a more normal market response than would be the case if consumers knew the product was being tested.

Internationally, test marketing may be more difficult to administer. Retailer cooperation is generally required, and retailers in many countries do not have the same close ties with manufacturers that characterize distribution channels in the United States. However, test marketing internationally is not unheard of, and in fact one country may be used as a "test" for an entire region. In the United States, where Coca-Cola is the Number One selling soft drink, a new product called Cherry Coke was introduced. Their major market competitor, Pepsi-Cola, immediately introduced their cherry cola under the Slice family brand to U.S. markets, but introduced their Cherry Pepsi in Canada, where Pepsi-Cola is the Number One soft drink. If successful in Canada, Cherry Pepsi may then be introduced to U.S. markets. Similarly, some multinational marketers use Uruguay as a test market for the rest of Latin America. Beatrice Foods launched a line of cheese, peanut, and chocolate snack foods; General Foods tested Tang; and Eastman Kodak introduced its disc camera and film in Uruguay before expanding to other parts of Latin America. These MNCs feel that testing a new product in small markets will keep potential losses to a minimum should a product or marketing program prove unsuccessful or need additional adaptation for profitable sales.[6]

Deciding to Conduct Primary Research

Primary research is designed to answer questions remaining after secondary data have been exhausted. It focuses on much more specific issues which are beyond the scope of published information. The costs of conducting international primary research, measured in both time and money (and including the problems inherent in multicountry research), must be weighed against the benefits. The benefits are of course the advantages that accrue from a more knowledgeable approach to the market. Considering the long-term nature and high capital investment frequently associated with international marketing, the research investment may be well worth it.

Many executives may allow their SRC to interfere when performing this cost-benefit analysis. That is, global marketing research is generally more expensive than a comparable domestic study due to the specialized services required, travel costs, and difficulty in obtaining data. Marketers may allow this higher cost to be a psychological barrier, avoiding marketing research until after a blunder has been made. It also indicates that more research tends to be done by the largest MNCs who have the resources to fund such research, when in fact small and medium-sized firms have research needs just as great. Finally, the big spenders in marketing research tend to be the United States, Canada, and Europe. Currently, total expenditures on marketing research worldwide averages about $2.75 billion annually. Of this, $1.35 billion is spent in North America, $1 billion in Europe, yet only $270 million is spent in Oceania/Asia, $40 million in Africa, and $20 million in the Middle East.[7] In deciding to conduct international marketing research marketers must eliminate the SRC and include in their analysis long-term market potential and the opportunity costs of *not* conducting research.

CONDUCTING INTERNATIONAL MARKETING RESEARCH

There are several alternatives available to a firm regarding who will conduct international marketing research. Large corporations with experience in global marketing probably have the resources and internal capabilities to conduct international market research. Hiring independent research firms may be more cost effective for smaller companies or for companies newly entering international markets. Other firms may use a combination of in-house research staff supplemented by outside research firms. These companies may find that their in-house marketing research departments are capable of the initial research involving secondary data, but lack the experience for primary data collection. Multicountry primary research involves familiarity with the local research environment and competence in multiple languages which few but the largest, most experienced have available in-house.

In recent years the number of firms providing quality international marketing research services has increased. These firms vary in price and services offered. A. C. Nielsen (U.S. based), the largest global market research company (in terms of sales) with offices in 22 countries, specializes in retail store audit data and test marketing. IMS International (U.S. parent), the second largest in terms of sales, has offices in 57 countries and specializes by product area—they are the predominant pharmaceutical researchers. Market Behavior (U.K.) specializes in qualitative research techniques, such as focus groups and projective techniques. Research International (U.K.) is one of the largest full-service market research companies, with offices in 29 countries.

SUMMARY

The success of an international marketing plan depends upon well-conceived, well-implemented, and thoughtfully analyzed market research. Sound decisions require complete and relevant information. The international marketing research environment is far more complex than the domestic situation, but with careful and creative application, the same objectives and procedures can be utilized.

This first section has introduced some of the more general concepts in international marketing. Hopefully it has provided insight into the differences and problems encountered by marketers adapting to a global environment. The following chapters will discuss more specific concepts relating to adapting the elements of the marketing mix to international markets.

EXERCISE 3–1

So you speak English. One of the problems in international marketing research is to communicate accurately with those in a research survey. We probably all accept the difficulty in communicating between English- and Japanese-speaking people, but how about English to English? The English speak English; North Americans speak English; but can we communicate?

Below are lists of words, expressions, and phrases used in England and in the United States. See if you can match each British word, expression, or phrase with the equivalent American word, expression, or phrase. There are more American words than British. The answers are listed in reverse order at the bottom of the exercise. Don't peek.

British	Your Choice
1. Cupboard	_____
2. Spend a penny	_____
3. Ladder	_____
4. Queer	_____
5. Crackers	_____
6. Knocked up	_____
7. Block of flats	_____
8. Braces	_____
9. Boot sale	_____

American

a. Go to the rest room	i. Run in a stocking
b. Crazy	j. Feel funny
c. Clothes closet	k. Saltines
d. Ill	l. Wake up call
e. Struck with a fist	m. Apartment house
f. China cabinet	n. Suspenders
g. Save on a purchase	o. Braces (teeth)
h. Garage sale	p. Shoe sale

(Answers are: c, a, i, j, b, l, m, n, h)

NOTES

1. Susan P. Douglas and C. Samuel Craig, *International Marketing Research* (Englewood Cliffs, N.J.: Prentice-Hall, 1983), p. 13.

2. David A. Ricks, *Big Business Blunders* (Homewood, Ill.: Dow Jones-Irwin, 1983), p. 105.

3. Douglas, *International Marketing Research,* p. 13.

4. Ibid., p. 139.

5. Ricks, *Big Business Blunders,* p. 68.

6. "Uruguay: Latin America's Favorite Test Market," *Advertising Age,* January 30, 1984, p. 52.

7. "Locating U.S. Foreign Trade Data," *Business America,* October 14, 1985, pp. 5–7.

CHAPTER FOUR

International Product Strategy

Once a firm recognizes an international opportunity—potential demand matched with available company resources—changes in the firm's marketing mix must be considered. The pivotal element is product planning. Simply stated, a successful product satisfies the wants and needs of the consumer. Only if the correct product decisions are made such that the product chosen does satisfy the needs of the consumer, will the consumer buy it. Obviously, only if the customer buys the product can the firm be profitable.

This chapter will introduce some of the key issues to consider when making international product decisions. The emphasis is on analysis rather than idea generation. Ideas for new products can come from any number of sources but it is only through careful screening and analysis that ideas turn into successful products. As you will see, many international product failures might have been prevented with more thoughtful planning. In some cases, astute marketers removed the product from the market early enough to successfully revise the marketing plan and reintroduce the product. For others a weak product decision was not detected in time to avoid losses to the firm. A poorly conceived product can leave a lasting negative impression on the market that may be difficult if not impossible to change. In addition, a poor product can potentially damage the reputation of other products in the line. For this reason, we shall be emphasizing well-planned adaptation of products to international markets to prevent, rather than cure, marketing errors.

HOME COUNTRY PRODUCT PLANNING

Even in domestic marketing, product planning is the central element. A product is more than just a physical entity; to marketers it represents a "bundle of satisfactions" for the consumer. As such it may be transformed in any number of ways to suit the needs of its target market. One of the best examples can be taken from the automobile industry. Before the advent of the marketing concept, American industry's fascination with production was epitomized by Henry Ford's statement "we'll give them any color they want as long as it's black." Now Ford produces annual model changes offering countless variations of styling, color, performance, luxury features, and price tailored to the consumer. American marketers recognized the advantages gained by adapting products both to suit the needs of their target market and to differentiate their product from the competition. There must be a balance, however, between producing what the company wants regardless of consumer needs and producing so many variations that product cost escalates to the point that some market segments are priced out of the market. Thus, when a product is evaluated as a potential candidate for international export, the decision whether to adapt the product to the overseas target market is made with this same concept of balance in mind. As you read this chapter, imagine yourself in the position of the international product manager who must answer these questions: Will product changes stimulate greater demand for the product even at a higher price? Or, will the product in its current form be satisfactory, perhaps necessitating changes in other areas of the marketing mix?

INTERNATIONAL PRODUCT PLANNING

This basic marketing concept, product planning, can be transferred to international markets: International marketers must also design products to satisfy the needs of their consumers. As you might expect, there are added complications in doing so. We shall approach this complex issue by first discussing some of the general factors that must be considered when attempting to assess the needs of a foreign market. In particular we will review the searching nature of the questions that a marketer must be prepared to ask and the misleading effect that the self-reference criterion may sometimes have on the analysis of the answers. Once the needs of foreign consumers are assessed, the more pragmatic analysis of the impact of other foreign uncontrollable elements must be conducted. Following this general overview, the Extended Product Model will be discussed as a framework to guide our investigation of the more specific areas of product adaptation. Consistent with our approach in previous chapters, we shall distinguish between mandatory changes dictated by legal or governmental forces and discretionary changes initiated by the marketer to better satisfy the consumer.

New Questions

Product planning for an international market involves anticipating the needs and wants of consumers in entirely different cultures and determining how those needs and wants might be satisfied by the firm's products. Answering such questions as Who uses the product? How and when is the product used? Where and how often is it purchased? as well as determining the value and importance of the various product features may be very different for a foreign market than for the U.S. market. Learning to ask the right questions rather than relying on past experiences gained in other, culturally different markets is as important to international product planning as finding the answers.

One approach to international product planning that has proved successful is the procedure followed by the Nestle Company. Each product manager has a country fact book that includes, along with a thorough analysis of the country environment, a variety of culturally related questions. In Germany, for example, the product manager for coffee must furnish answers to the following questions: How does a German rank coffee in the hierarchy of consumer products? Is Germany a high or low per capita consumption market? (In Sweden annual per capita consumption of coffee is 18 pounds; in Japan it is half a gram!) How is coffee used—in bean form, ground, or powdered? If it is ground, how is it brewed? Which coffee is preferred—Brazilian Santos blended with Colombian coffee or robusta from the Ivory Coast? Is it roasted? Do the people prefer dark roasted or blond coffee? (Nestle's soluble coffee must match the *color* of local brewed coffee.) Do the Germans drink coffee after lunch or with breakfast? Do they take it black or with cream or milk? Do they drink coffee in the evening? Do they sweeten it? At what age do people begin drinking coffee? Is it a traditional beverage, as in France, or is it a form of rebellion, as in England and Japan, where the younger generation has taken up coffee in order to defy their tea-drinking parents?[1]

As you can tell from this partial example, there are a great many questions to be asked about a seemingly simple product. Questions like those about coffee must be asked for each product in every country in which the product is marketed. The same question, asked in Japan, France, Mexico, or some other country, may result in different answers thus requiring a "different" product to fit different market needs. Asking the right questions can mean the difference between product success and product failure.

Self-Reference Criterion

In Chapter 1 we introduced the problem of the self-reference criterion (SRC); that is, using the home country frame of reference while making decisions about foreign markets. The following example of the two American cake mix companies attempting to enter the U.K. market, first mentioned in Chapter 1, illustrates the problem of SRC in international product planning.

As you may recall, Company A, the undisputed American leader in cake mixes, failed to introduce profitably to the British market its successful easy cake mixes from the U.S. market. Company B, on the other hand, also an American company, was successful in Britain with a simple, very popular dry sponge cake mix. What was the difference in the market approaches of these two companies?

Company A executives evidently relied on their SRC in assuming that the most popular American cakes would also be popular in Britain. In fact, the British eat most of their cakes with tea, not for dessert. The fancy iced cakes that Americans favor are generally considered extra special in Britain and are purchased from a bakery or "made from scratch" at home. Company A introduced their "easy" mix that was very popular with Americans, but the British felt it was just not good enough for these special occasions. Company B executives had not relied on their (American) SRC but instead investigated the British market. They found that the most popular cake was a dry sponge cake and introduced that as an easy cake mix. Not surprisingly, by making a product for which the British expressed a need, Company B was quite successful.[2]

This example demonstrates not only the problems caused by the marketers' reliance on their SRC, but that the problem of SRC can be overcome. Careful product planning in the early stages can prevent costly errors, like the one described above, later in the marketing process.

Uncontrollable Elements

As we discussed in Chapter 2, the number and the complexity of uncontrollable environmental forces increase when entering an international market. Legal, political, and governmental elements may impose mandatory (uncontrolled by the marketer) product changes. Cultural, economic, technological, geographic, or competitive influences will most likely indicate discretionary (controlled by the marketer) product changes. The nature and extent of these changes will vary country by country and product to product. Each time the MNC (multinational corporation) analyzes the decision to enter a foreign market, the international product manager must evaluate these foreign uncontrollable elements and the various ways in which they could affect the product. The decision can then be made as to what kinds of changes will be implemented, if any.

Product Adaptation

Given the myriad of foreign uncontrollable elements, the marketer's self-reference criterion, and all of the other variables that complicate product analysis, how does the marketer come to a product decision? One effective decision-making tool for product adaptation is the extended product model, which systematically categorizes all tangible and intangible elements of the product. By evaluating each product level, from the tangible physical core product through the packaging components and the more intangible support components, the product planner can be relatively assured of considering all pertinent variables. Remember as you go through the model that the marketer will look at mandatory changes first, then will consider discretionary changes. Keep in mind that the marketing manager is not necessarily seeking to make changes for change's sake but to make those changes that will enhance the value of the product to the consumer. Generally speaking, the fewer product changes made the better since economies of scale in production, multicountry product recognition, the levels of international product inventories, and international distribution can all be improved with a standardized product. However, changes are sometimes required, and it is this decision that we shall now investigate.

EXTENDED PRODUCT MODEL

As students of marketing, you are aware that the product is more than just its physical components. The extended product model, which aids marketers in visualizing what is meant by that concept, is shown in Exhibit 4–1.

When marketers speak of the "product," they refer not only to the core component, but to the packaging and support components as well. Let us now analyze each part of the overall product in light of the environmental influences presented in the previous sections to identify potential areas for either mandatory or discretionary product change.

Core Component

The key question to ask with regard to the core product is: What need will the product satisfy? The answer to that question will be the basis for all further product decisions, just as product planning decisions will be the basis for the rest of the marketing mix. Marketers must not rely on their SRC to answer the question, but must answer from the host country perspective. For example, we know that a bicycle is more than spoked wheels, handlebars, and a seat. For an American, a bicycle may be used for recreation, for exercise, for family outings, for fun and

EXHIBIT 4–1 Extended Product Model

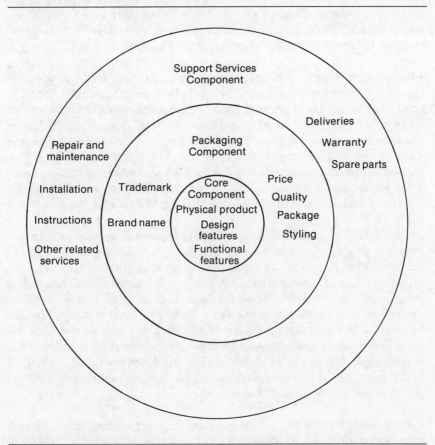

Support Services Component

Packaging Component

Core Component

Physical product

Design features

Functional features

Price

Quality

Package

Styling

Trademark

Brand name

Repair and maintenance

Installation

Instructions

Other related services

Deliveries

Warranty

Spare parts

fresh air, for sport, or for competition. Even status needs can be satisfied: Witness the students who ride $600 European touring bikes from the dorms to class. Contrast a consumer in the PRC (People's Republic of China) who may use a bicycle as transportation for himself, or to transport small amounts of goods. Depending on the need that the bicycle is intended to satisfy, the consumer will place a different value and importance on the various product components. The American wants a lightweight, fast bicycle, perhaps with various status features, whereas the Chinese may want a sturdier, more stable bicycle to withstand the rigors of basic transportation and light hauling. These differing needs between the two consumers may require changes in each of the three parts of the core component: physical product, functional features, and design features. There may also be need to make changes in the other two product components (packaging component and support services component) as well. Discretionary changes might be made by the marketer to bring the product more in line with consumer needs, while mandatory changes may be required by the host country before the product is permitted to enter.

Physical Product.   One example of such a discretionary change in the physical product follows. The Campbell Soup Company found it easier to change their product than to change the habits of consumers when marketing canned soup in Great Britain. They first introduced Campbell's condensed soups, their U.S. standard for the past 50 years.[3] Though priced competitively, the British were unfamiliar with condensed soups and believed that Campbell's was offering half as much soup for twice as much money. To correct the problem, Campbell's hurriedly added water and enlarged the can to look like the rest of the soups on the shelf.

It is not unusual for mandatory changes to be required in the physical product for a variety of reasons, such as avoiding nontariff barriers. The Japanese, for example, have strict quality standards on all goods entering the country. Similarly, the United States has safety regulations and restrictions on emissions for automobiles with which foreign as well as domestic car manufacturers must comply. The differences in driving laws between the United States and the U.K. require automobile producers to change the placement of the steering mechanism. These are not insurmountable barriers to marketing in these countries, but represent situations where mandatory product changes are a prerequisite to market entry.

Functional Features.   The geographic environment can dictate mandatory changes in the functional features of a product. General Motors of Canada experienced major problems when it shipped 13,500 Chevrolet Malibu automobiles to Iraq, only to discover that they were unfit for the hot, dusty climate. Iraq refused shipment of the remaining 12,000 autos; GM tripled the numbers of engineers and mechanics in Baghdad. By the time GM discovered that supplementary air filters and different clutches would solve the problem, political problems had put an end to the deal. At last report, 12,000 automobiles specially designed for desert driving were collecting snow in Canada.

Discretionary changes in a product's functional features might be made when the product manager believes the changes will lead to increased demand for the product. For example, time-saving features in a product would increase its appeal to a U.S. market, while another culture would be indifferent to that product feature. One discussion of the relevance of primary and secondary functional features of a product to international marketing uses the refrigerator as an example.[4] In the United States, the primary function of a refrigerator is to keep frozen foods frozen and to preserve perishables. Secondary functional features are many. We use the refrigerator for storage, to make ice, and to keep drinks cold. As a result, Americans desire large refrigerators with plenty of storage capacity, a larger freezer, and even ice-making and ice water features on the door. Our time-saving culture would also value a self-defrosting feature. All of these discretionary changes are made to the U.S. version of the product to enhance the demand and more specifically meet consumer needs for both the primary and secondary functional features. Internationally, however, consumers may only have a need for a refrigerator's primary function— to keep perishables. Because of cultural differences such as frequent shopping, preference for drinking room-temperature liquids, and eating fresh rather than frozen foods, consumers may not be willing to pay for the storage space, ice-making function, or large freezer space. Thus the marketer might make discretionary changes in the product's functional features to appeal to international markets with different cultural values.

Design Features.   Any number of environmental factors might indicate changes in product design features. Competition, cultural aesthetics, economic conditions, legal and governmental requirements, and level of technology might individually or collectively influence design. Airplane design in the United States and the United Kingdom provides an interesting illustration. American firms, concerned with the high cost of labor, designed their planes with the engines suspended from the wings. This was less aerodynamically efficient but easier to get at for repairs and servicing. British firms were more concerned with conservation of fuel, and implanted the engines within the wing design for maximum fuel efficiency. In this example it is clear that external environmental factors influenced the design objectives of the engineers, and these factors were quite different in each country.

Packaging Component

The packaging component involves both tangible and intangible elements including style features, packaging, labeling, trademark, brand name, quality, and price. As with the core component, the importance of each of these elements in the eyes of the consumer depends upon the need that the product is designed to serve. If status or prestige needs are to be satisfied, brand names and labels become increasingly important. If fashion or aesthetic needs must be satisfied, the style and design features should be emphasized. Besides these discretionary changes, international product managers must frequently make changes in packaging and labeling to meet governmental or environmental constraints.

Trademark.   An important issue in international marketing is the protection of intellectual property rights, such as trademarks, brand names, patents, and copyrights. In the United States—a common-law country like England and her former colonies—ownership of intellectual property rights is established by prior use. In fact, before trademarks and brand names can be registered, they must be in use. In code-law countries (remember that code law is based on an all-inclusive system of written rules), the first to register a trademark is the rightful owner. Though registered ownership may be challenged based upon proof of prior use in the market, there have been instances of U.S. companies buying back legal ownership of their own trademarks or brand names.

Trademarks may also be inadvertently offensive or misinterpreted. One company whose red circle trademark is popular in many countries ran into trouble in some parts of Asia where it conjured up images of the Japanese flag.[5] Flowers can also have different meanings. Yellow flowers mean death or disrespect in Mexico and mean infidelity in France and the Soviet Union. Care must be taken to ensure that corporate trademarks do not carry hidden meanings.

Brand Names.   Branding is an important decision in international markets just as it is in domestic marketing, and for many similar reasons. Some advantages to using the same brand name internationally include the following: establishment of a corporate image that acts as a base for later expansion of the product line; consistency in advertising and promotion, particularly where media broadcasts cross national boundaries; and greater recognition by international travelers. The disadvantages are similar to those problems identified domestically: poor quality control may damage the brand image; a poorly chosen brand name may inhibit additions to the line (such as when Hotpoint appliances added a refrigerator to their line of appliances).

Some countries require that brand names be an accurate description of the product. For example, Canada's "Cherry Pepsi" would have to be renamed "Cherry-flavored Pepsi" in South Korea, since the product contains no actual cherries. More frequently, international marketers have been plagued with translation problems. When Coca-Cola went into China, translators chose characters that sounded phonetically like Coca-Cola; they actually read "bite the wax tadpole." Needless to say, the company changed the characters. Ford introduced a low-cost truck in Mexico under the brand name Fiera. Unfortunately, in Spanish *fiera* means "ugly old woman." Even more embarrassing was their top-of-the-line Caliente, which is slang for "streetwalker" in some Spanish-speaking countries. Americans are not the only ones to make these international *faux pas:* the Japanese have tried to market a "Skinababe" baby soap and a "Blow Up" hair care product in the United States.[6]

Packaging. Mandatory changes in product packaging may be indicated after analyzing the legal, governmental, and economic requirements of the host country. Many countries in the world use the metric system of measurement and will require U.S. firms to conform to those standards. According to a recent study, most MNCs expect less developed countries to begin legislating package sizes to reduce confusion among unsophisticated consumers. Manufacturers in Kenya, Singapore, and Malaysia must now conform to government standards for bottle, can, and packaged food sizes. In countries with low per capita incomes products such as cigarettes, razor blades, and chewing gum are sold in small or individual units so that consumers can afford to buy them. Warner-Lambert sells Chiclets brand name chewing gum in a two-piece pack for a few cents in Latin America, rather than the 12-piece pack sold in the United States.

Analysis of local culture, local geography, and the host country distribution system often leads to discretionary product changes. A British firm marketing tea biscuits in Asia would have been well advised to make a simple package change dictated by cultural preference. The firm's product was introduced in its traditional white package; however, because white is the color of mourning in Asia, the product was not well received. A change to a red package might have saved the product, since red is very popular in Oriental culture, but the firm refused to "break tradition" and the product was removed from the market. Geography will also impact packaging: Quaker Oats, for example, uses special vacuum-sealed tins to protect its products sold in hot and humid climates. Geographic conditions unfavorable to product shelf-life can be even more problematic when local distribution is slow. Though distribution in major urban areas is generally comparable throughout the world, the number and efficiency of distributors drops outside urban areas. In some instances it may be more cost effective to augment the sales force and build distributor relationships rather than increase product cost further with elaborate protective packaging.

Labeling. Firms are often unaware that labeling laws in many countries are even more demanding than in the United States. In Saudi Arabia, for example, specific product names are required; "hot chili" is insufficient if the product is *"spiced* hot chili." Also compulsory are a list of ingredients, net weight of contents (in metric units), manufacturer's name and address, date of manufacture, and product-use expiration date, all of which must be printed in both Arabic and English.

MNCs who try to simplify product distribution by supplying multiple markets from a single regional manufacturing facility may be frustrated in their attempt by the need to comply with different labeling laws in each country. In Venezuela, for example, prices must be printed on the labels; in Chile it is illegal for manufacturers to put prices on labels or to even suggest retail prices.

The symbols used on labels must also be chosen with care. The classic example of misinterpreted symbols was experienced by Gerber baby foods. They introduced their traditional small jars of baby food in Africa complete with labels featuring the picture of the Gerber baby. The company was amazed to find that consumers were absolutely horrified—they thought that the jars contained ground-up babies. Though this may seem to be a far-fetched example, this type of misunderstanding is not all that uncommon in low-literacy cultures where consumers must rely on symbols and pictures for instructions and information.

Styling. Cultural aesthetics greatly influence the consumer's perceived value of a product, and in particular will influence product styling. For example, the Scandanavians are renowned for their sleek functional styling of home furnishings which have become increasingly popular in the United States in recent years. Timing of style changes is crucial however, as any follower of fashion knows. Olivetti learned this lesson the hard way in the 1960s when they attempted to introduce to the U.S. market a new typewriter with a sleek, European award-winning design. American consumers thought it too "flimsy," equating bigness and bulk with durability and quality. (Remember slamming car doors to see how solid a new car was?) Today American consumers would probably love such a design.

Support Services Component

Adaptations of the support services component of the product can increase the product's value in the perception of the consumer as well. Again, some changes are mandatory while others are discretionary, but all changes are made in the context of satisfying consumer needs. Support services include repair and maintenance, instructions, installation, warranties, deliveries, and availability of spare parts.

Repair and Maintenance. The general economic level of the country, its degree of service orientation, the concept of time and leisure, and the culture's materialistic values are some of the factors that might influence the country's perception of product repair and maintenance.

Certainly no one wants a product that is in frequent need of repair, but the question becomes one of do-it-yourself versus servicing. U.S. consumers have large discretionary incomes, are extremely time-conscious, and value their leisure time. Not surprisingly they have become increasingly service-oriented. In any community there are a number of competitive service retailers ready to repair and maintain anything from your automobile to your television set. As amazing as it may seem to the rest of the world, U.S. consumers even consider some products, such as small household appliances, to be virtually disposable. When the toaster breaks, we throw it away and buy a new one! The time and effort involved in getting it repaired is greater than the minimal cost of replacing it. Indeed many U.S. products warn consumers *not* to attempt self-repair.

On the contrary, many poorer countries perceive self-repair as not only desirable but necessary. In an amusing article on global economic development, Farmer measured industrialization by the degree of accumulated "junk." Underdeveloped and semideveloped nations have little or no junk since all product components are continually recycled. Industrialized countries are evidenced by a continuously increasing accumulation of "junk," as the disposable society takes over. Incomes reach a level where the consumers would rather buy a new item than fix the old one (e.g., the toaster). Interestingly, postindustrial societies are once again evidenced by less junk, as ecological and environmental concerns stimulate recycling.[7]

Some semideveloped and newly industrialized countries are unfamiliar with the concept of product maintenance. Americans working in the PRC are amazed to find Chinese workers completely oblivious to the routine maintenance needs of trucks and other machinery. PRC workers will drive on flat tires, ignore levels of engine fluids, and generally "run vehicles into the ground." Machine tolerances must be increased for these consumers; perhaps maintenance servicing should be provided with the product. Japan has addressed the problem by designing a maintenance-free vehicle for the PRC market.

Instructions.   Literacy rates and educational levels of a country may cause a firm to change a product's usage instructions. What might seem like a "simple" term may be incomprehensible to locals. For example, rural Africans had trouble understanding that Vaseline Intensive Care lotion is "absorbed" into the skin. Chesebrough-Pond's changed the wording to "soaks into" to alleviate confusion.

Some companies with an eye to the future, like Lever Brothers, invest in rural promotions to educate consumers about product use. This strategy pays off when rural inhabitants become regular wage earners, since they buy brands familiar to them. Other consumer goods companies use movies to advertise products and to demonstrate product use. In between feature films, commercials—often 10 to 20 minutes long—show what detergent or toothpaste is and how to use it.

Sometimes unfamiliarity with product terms can lead to humorous translations of instructions. One computer firm hired an Indonesian exchange student to translate an instruction booklet for customers in Djakarta. The term *software* was translated in various places in the booklet as *underwear, tissue,* and *computer junk*. Needless to say this caused some consternation among consumers attempting to use the product. Legal restrictions in Nicaragua, Iraq, Thailand, and Saudi Arabia require bilingual or trilingual instructions. The Nestle infant formula case* convinced many LDCs to require not only multilingual instructions, but also pictorial instructions for those who cannot read.

Regardless of company instructions for intended product use, some international customers perceive the product as satisfying other needs. In rural Africa, the skin protection features of petroleum jelly are second to its cosmetic appeal. Because they find it beautiful, Africans apply petroleum jelly everywhere on the body, except the face. As another example, a manufacturer of sanitary napkins sent a representative to South America to investigate particularly good sales results. Imagine the manufacturer's representative's surprise when he discovered consumers were farm workers using the product as dust masks in the fields. Despite corporate intentions, some consumers will persist in using the product as they see fit. Perhaps the astute marketer will see further product opportunities from such events.

Extended Product Model: Summary

This section has discussed in some detail the extended product model as a useful framework for international marketers analyzing the match between the needs and wants of prospective overseas customers and the product offerings of the firm. By evaluating the core component, the packaging component, and the support services component of the product, the marketer can determine the elements that require adaptation for acceptance in foreign markets and the elements that can be exported successfully without change. The remaining sections of this chapter present a number of additional issues that are critical to making sound international product planning decisions.

STANDARDIZED VERSUS DIFFERENTIATED PRODUCTS

Upon completing the product analysis and integrating the perceived needs of the target market with the mandatory requirements of the

---

*See chapter 8 for a discussion of the Nestle case.

various uncontrollable environmental elements, the marketer must now decide upon the exact product to satisfy consumer needs, within the given environmental constraints and at a profit to the firm. Essentially there are but three alternatives: (1) select a product from the firm's current product line; (2) modify a current product to suit the individual needs of the target market; or (3) develop a totally new product. In this section we shall look at the advantages and disadvantages of each option and see some examples of each strategy in action.

Standardization

The degree of change introduced in consumer goods depends not only on cultural and economic differences between home country markets and host countries, but also on multinational corporations' international product policies. Many MNCs have basic product groups that are standardized worldwide. Such "flagship" products as Coca-Cola, Colgate toothpaste, Canada Dry mixers, and Pond's cold cream give their respective companies global images.[8] These products are usually the first introduced into new markets and act as the foundation for developing locally oriented product lines. Good candidates for standardization are products that are not culturally sensitive such as industrial products or consumer durables, and consumer products like baby diapers or razor blades, whose use patterns are the same throughout the world. Industrial goods such as component parts or raw materials that become part of an end product are usually standardized for production facilities worldwide.

Standardized products are desirable because significant cost savings and production efficiencies can be obtained. Yet, economies of scale in production are of no value if there is insufficient demand for the product in its current form. Cost-benefit analysis must look closely at the cost savings obtained with standardization in light of the potential increase in market demand generated by adapting the product to local tastes.

Differentiation

In the product adaptation section we analyzed myriad possible product changes in light of the external environmental influences that might require those changes. How do marketers decide if, and how many, changes should be made? First, mandatory product changes are made to make the product conform to legal, governmental, and economic requirements. These usually involve measurements, packaging, and labeling changes. Next, discretionary changes are made. These are generally based on aesthetics, consumer preferences, and competition. A recent study reported that nearly 7 out of 10 changes made by MNCs in transposing a product to LDCs are implemented to satisfy local market preference.[9]

Finally, changes must be evaluated from a profitability standpoint. The added demand generated by product modifications must be weighed against a possible increase in price to cover the costs of those changes. If the cost of added changes is too high, then the product may be dropped and a totally new product developed.

Who makes these product decisions? The issue of how companies come to these new product decisions will be discussed in the next section on new product development.

NEW PRODUCT DEVELOPMENT

The aforementioned study found that more than half the products the MNCs sell in the LDCs originate in the companies' home markets; local managers typically select products to be transferred from worldwide product lines. Sometimes the product is accepted without change, like Coca-Cola or Gillette razor blades which need little or no modification to adapt to local conditions. Frequently, however, MNCs entering LDC markets find that their current product line is too sophisticated or technologically advanced for local markets. In this case, product simplification may be indicated. Products designed for high-speed, precision operations necessary in the United States or other industrialized countries may be redesigned for lower output, easier maintenance, and simpler operations to make the product a better technological fit to local needs. For example, a computer-operated milling machine that produces 10,000 bolts per hour may be too costly and complicated for a market where the need is for only 10,000 bolts per week. A redesigned, lower-priced bolt machine may be more appropriate than the high-speed, computer-operated one sold in more developed markets.

Great care must be taken not to offend the host culture when using this approach. What may seem to the MDC marketer like transfer of "appropriate technology" will often be interpreted by the LDC as "imperialistic paternalism." MDC marketers tend not to realize that while LDCs may be poor, they are not totally unaware of the latest technology. They will often demand "state of the art" technology so as not to seem backward, even if that may not objectively appear to be the "best" product given the situation. Tact is a most valuable marketing tool in such an instance.

Other times product modifications are so extensive that essentially a new product designed specifically for the international market must be developed. This approach is the most expensive, time-consuming, and risky strategy and is undertaken only if the market demand justifies the cost. For example, food companies such as Pillsbury, Swift, and Coca-Cola have developed high-protein foods to sell in foreign countries as diet supplements and have met with reasonable success. However, both General Motors Corporation and Ford Motor Company developed a "bare bones" Model T-type vehicle to sell in developing countries; both products failed. The General Motors' product, a truck designed for the Far East, lost out to the low prices on used passenger cars which were converted to utility vehicles. The local market felt the GM product was too sophisticated and costly. On the other hand, Ford's attempt to develop an "Asian People's Car" failed for just the opposite reason: The demand was for more sophisticated and more expensive Japanese vehicles.

Regardless of whether a current product is being modified or a totally new product is being developed for the international market, the product manager will probably take it through the six-step new product development process. The process starts with an *idea:* It can be an idea for a new product or for ways to adapt and internationally market an existing product. The ideas are then *screened and evaluated* to determine which ones merit further study. Those that survive are subjected to a *business analysis* to estimate market potential and profitability. Up to this point the product team is concept testing. In international marketing these phases are extremely important, because as we know from domestic marketing, the next phases are expensive, difficult, and time-consuming. Most new product ideas never make it this far. Those that do then go into *product development* where the "on paper" idea starts to become a physical reality. If the production of the new product is seen as operationally and financially feasible, the product may be *test marketed.* As we saw in the marketing research chapter, this step is often omitted in international marketing because international distributors are largely unfamiliar with test marketing and the product manager may have a difficult time in gaining middleman cooperation. If all goes well, the new product goes into *commercialization* and the rest of the marketing mix is tailored around it.

NEW PRODUCT INTRODUCTION

The "new product" may be considered "new" in a number of ways. The product may be simply new to the firm, but one that is already made available by competitors in the market. Alternately, the product may be new to the market. In either case, it is the consumer's perception of the newness of the product that is the focus of all subsequent marketing decisions. Pricing, distribution, and particularly promotional planning will all be influenced by consumer perceptions of newness. Therefore, it will be important for the marketer to know *how new* the product is to the consumer. Is it a new product type or simply a new brand? Will it require new behavior on the part of the consumer to utilize the product effectively, or will it fit into present consumption patterns?

The term *congruent innovations* is applied to innovations that require no changes at all—for example, New Coke versus Classic Coke. *Continuous innovations* involve alteration of a product currently in use. They are usually minimally disruptive to behavior patterns, such as the introduction of fluoride in toothpaste to a country where toothpaste is regularly used. Remember, however, that the determination of how disruptive the innovation is, is made by the host culture, not the MNC marketing division. The rejection of filter-tipped cigarettes in Asia provides a case in point. In areas where life expectancies hover around 40 years, lung disease is a low-priority concern. No product improvement was perceived by the consumers, and the product was not adopted. At the other end of the scale, a *discontinuous* innovation requires the establishment of new consumption patterns. It introduces an idea or behavior pattern where there was none before. Examples in the United States include the introduction of television, automobiles, and computers, which have had a far-reaching impact on consumer behavior.[10]

The degree of newness perceived by the market will influence how the product is marketed. For example, for a product perceived as a discontinuous innovation in the overseas market, the firm may decide to plan for an extended introductory period in order to create awareness for the new product and to generate primary demand (demand for the product type). Adoption of the product may be relatively slow, and expenditures for advertising and promotion commensurately high. A product already familiar to the market such as a congruent innovation requires a different approach than a discontinuous innovation. In this case the firm could immediately begin to stimulate secondary demand or demand for the firm's brand, since the product type would already be known to consumers. The international marketer must always consider the possibility that a product perceived as a congruent innovation in the home market could be perceived as a discontinuous innovation in a foreign market, and changes to the marketing mix would be evaluated accordingly.

In addition to the degree of perceived newness the product enjoys in the overseas market, the marketer must also realize that the product is, in all likelihood, in the introductory stages of the product life cycle. The marketer must consider the stage of product life cycle and the speed with which the product will move through its life cycle when making international product decisions.

PRODUCT LIFE CYCLE

International marketers frequently take a product that is in the maturity or decline stage of the product life cycle in the United States and extend the life of the product by introducing it to new, international markets. In many of those countries, it must be remembered that the product will probably be in a different stage of the product life cycle than in the United States. If this is the case, pricing strategy, distribution strategy, and promotional strategy must be changed to reflect this "reincarnated" stage of the product life cycle.

One company that neglected to consider this was Polaroid, when introducing the Swinger camera to the French market. After 20 years of success with the instant camera, Polaroid introduced the Model 20 "Swinger" Land Camera to a mature U.S. market in 1965. After a phenomenally successful introduction in the United States, Polaroid introduced the Swinger in France using its "successful" (i.e., for a mature camera market) U.S. marketing program. The Swinger was Polaroid's first product in France, and a spectacular failure.

What happened? As far as the French market was concerned, not only the Swinger camera, but the very concept of instant photography were previously unknown. The product was in the introductory stage of its life cycle in France, yet Polaroid was using a marketing program designed for a mature U.S. market with 20 years of experience with instant cameras. Polaroid withdrew the Swinger, changed the marketing approach, and successfully reintroduced it.

SUMMARY

Product planning decisions are the most central yet some of the most complex of the international marketing mix. The marketing manager must choose a product that satisfies the wants and needs of a culturally unique market, while observing environmentally imposed constraints and achieving profitability for the firm. Crucial to this process is the ability of the marketer to objectively perceive the product from the perspective of the consumer, recognizing that what may be a familiar product in one market may be an innovation to the consumer in another market.

EXERCISE 4–1

Select a product (a major household appliance such as a refrigerator, washing machine, or clothes dryer) that your firm will market. Using the Extended Product

Model (see Exhibit 4–1), interview a person from Japan or some other country and determine the adaptation necessary to successfully market the product in their country. Select someone who has only recently come to the United States. Write a short report indicating the changes you think have to be made, and identify those that are mandatory or discretionary.

NOTES

1. Philip R. Cateora, *International Marketing,* 6th. ed. (Homewood, Ill.: Richard D. Irwin, 1987), p. 447.

2. P. d'Antin, "The Nestle Product Manager as a Demigod," *European Business,* Spring 1971, pp. 44–49.

3. David A. Ricks, *Big Business Blunders* (Homewood, Ill.: Dow Jones-Irwin, 1983), p. 24.

4. John Fayerweather, *International Marketing* (Englewood Cliffs, N.J.: Prentice-Hall, 1970), p. 67.

5. Ricks, *Big Business Blunders,* p. 33.

6. Lennie Copeland and Lewis Griggs, *Going International* (New York: Random House, 1985).

7. Cateora, *International Marketing,* p. 323.

8. "World Brands," *Advertising Age,* June 25, 1984, p. 49.

9. John S. Hill and Richard R. Still, "Adapting Products to LDC Taste," *Harvard Business Review,* March–April 1984, pp. 95–98.

10. Thomas S. Robertson, "Determinants of Innovative Behavior," *Proceedings of the American Marketing Association,* ed. Reed Mayer (*American Marketing Association,* 1967), pp. 328–32.

CHAPTER FIVE

International Pricing

Pricing may well be the most sensitive area of the international marketing mix. The final price, or the price at which the product is offered to the ultimate consumer, contributes not only to the image of the product but to the overall image of the firm as well. For example, if the public believes that a product is priced too high, this will reflect negatively on the image of the product (they will not buy it) and also on the company as a whole ("the company is trying to reap excess profits"). Yet as crucial as pricing strategy is to the overall marketing plan, the American firm may find it difficult to control the prices of its products in international markets. Though the marketing department may be in control of the price as the product leaves the home country, it is not surprising to find that foreign environmental influences have made it necessary for the firm to change the price (generally, change it upward) several times before the product ever reaches the ultimate consumer.

Consistent with previous chapters, the emphasis is upon adaptations made voluntarily by the firm and adaptations mandated by the international environment in which the firm chooses to operate. In this chapter the focus is upon issues unique to international marketing which, in combination, will influence the determination of the final price of the product in foreign markets. The first half of the chapter examines the firm's pricing microenvironment; that is, the direct interaction between the firm (as represented by the product) and the consumer. International pricing issues within the control of the firm and instrumental in setting the product's targeted final price are examined. As in domestic marketing, the goal is to set a price that will stimulate consumer demand while satisfying the financial objectives of management. However, the final price targeted by the firm may not be the final price offered to the consumer or received by the firm. The second half of the chapter is therefore devoted to the firm's pricing macroenvironment. The issues here are external to the firm, usually beyond the control of the firm, but nonetheless influence the product's final price. Topics covered in this section include analysis of the potential effects on the firm, and subsequently on the prices charged by the firm, of actions taken by international and local competitors, of legislation enacted by host governments, of changes in host country economic conditions, and of international financial considerations.

PRICE ESCALATION

When an American firm exports a product to international markets, the costs of transportation, packing, insurance, tariffs, taxes, storage fees, documentation costs, and middlemen margins are all added to the domestic cost basis* of the product. These additional costs, unique to the domestic firm attempting to enter international markets, combine to inflate the final price to a level considerably higher than the price charged in domestic markets. This cost disadvantage which causes price escalation is the first major obstacle that the foreign firm must overcome if it is to compete successfully in international markets.

An Example of Price Escalation

Following the progress of a product from its domestic origin to the foreign consumer will help to explain how price escalation happens. Let us assume that a product leaves the U.S. manufacturing plant at its normal domestic price. It will then incur freight and shipping costs to get it from, say, Kansas City to New York City and then from New York to Paris. At the port of entry in France, tariffs will be paid. These may be based on a percent of the value (ad valorem), be in the form of a flat fee (specific duty), or be a combination of both. The transactions necessary to get the product to France may be handled by a foreign freight forwarder who will add a fee for services. Legal fees will probably be incurred to handle documentation; insurance must be paid to offset the possibility of breakage and pilferage in the transatlantic crossing. Once the product passes through customs, paying all necessary customs fees (tariffs), port charges, documentation fees, and so forth, it must be unloaded and stored. Additional middlemen will handle the product as it is distributed to the final consumer, incurring more distribution costs. These host country middlemen include whole-

---

*The domestic cost basis refers to the total cost, to the domestic firm, of producing the product. It includes variable costs (such as materials and labor) and an allocation of fixed costs (overhead and administration).

salers, retailers, and transportation companies, each of whom generally adds a fixed percentage margin to the price paid for the product. It is easy to see how the foreign price might escalate to a level double or triple the domestic price. This higher "landed" price for the product may be entirely out of line with the prices of competing products or the prices of available substitutes. In this event, the net result would be severely limited or even nonexistent consumer demand for the product. The firm's initial strategic alternative, then, is to try to reduce the causes of price escalation.

Reducing Price Escalation

The key to reducing price escalation is to find ways to lower costs. There are several strategic approaches that companies can take to do this, some of which are discussed in the following sections. The firm may decide to make changes in the marketing mix to counteract the effects of price escalation. Changes in the physical product, in the distribution strategy, or in the promotional campaign may be implemented to offset the rising costs of getting the product to the foreign consumer. In addition, some governments have taken action to help foreign corporations reduce the landed cost of their imports.

Marketing Action.   The product itself might be changed to a less-expensive version to reduce the initial cost. Luxury features necessary to stimulate demand in sophisticated U.S. markets might be eliminated without negative consequences when the product is going to a more functionally oriented market. Special features on washing machines designed to dispense bleach or fabric softener automatically may be a costly addition whose elimination would not affect demand in the foreign market but would reduce costs. Affluent American consumers demand automobiles that not only provide performance, safety, and good gas mileage, but also superior styling, tinted glass windows, automatic transmissions, push-button windows and door locks, stereos, rear-window defoggers, burglar alarms—the list is endless. Elimination of these "luxurious" functional features or making them available in the form of options would lower the price of the basic automobile in a foreign market and would in all likelihood make its price more appealing to the target market.

Tariffs may be reduced by modifying the product in such a way that it can be reclassified at a different rate category. For example, one auto accessory company packaged its product with a wrench and an instruction booklet for foreign markets, changing its import category from the higher-tariff "accessory" to the lower tariff "tool."

Since tariffs are frequently lower for unassembled or partially manufactured goods, American exporters often ship components intended for assembly in a foreign country instead of fully finished products. Shipping components to be assembled by local and frequently lower-priced labor permits not only lower tariffs but perhaps lower total costs as well. The full extension of this cost-reduction approach is complete overseas production, which may be implemented if demand for the product and subsequent production cost savings justify the capital investment of building the overseas production facility.

Analysis of the product's channel of distribution may reveal where a channel member could be eliminated further reducing costs. Though the distribution function must still be performed, savings may be obtained by shortening distribution channels and making current channels more efficient.

One additional way a firm can reduce price escalation is to use variable cost pricing. Rather than assign full costs to the price of a product, firms charge only for the marginal or incremental costs of producing goods destined for export markets. Assuming the products sold abroad are the result of excess production capacity, these sales can be very profitable after break-even costs are reached even if full costs are not covered. The lower domestic base price may then enable the firm to price more competitively in the international market. There is a risk with this strategy because the firm is selling its product abroad at a lower net price than in the domestic market, and therefore may be subject to charges of dumping its product on the foreign market. This concept is discussed more completely later in this chapter.

Government Action.   Foreign-trade zones (FTZs) or free ports found in some countries are a help to the exporter seeking ways to reduce price escalation. There are more than 200 FTZs located throughout the world. More than 50 are located in the United States, including New York, New Orleans, San Francisco, Seattle, and Honolulu. Goods destined for a foreign market are shipped to a foreign trade zone in the importing country for storage or further processing. No tariffs or import duties are paid on the shipment until the product leaves the FTZ. If the finished goods are destined for importation by a third country, no import duty need be paid on those goods to the country where the FTZ is located. An additional advantage of processing goods in an FTZ is that all labor and other costs incurred in an FTZ are most often exempt from tariffs and taxes. Thus, goods entering an FTZ as unassembled will be taxed as unassembled rather than at the higher rate for fully assembled goods.[1]

By using an FTZ, a company can reduce price escalation considerably. Since tariffs can be paid as goods leave inventory rather than upon arrival to a country, considerable savings in inventory costs can be realized. Consider the extra cost of maintaining an average monthly inventory valued at $1 million on a product with a 25 percent ad valorem tax. By storing the inventory in an FTZ and deferring the tariffs until the products leave the zone, $250,000 less would be required to maintain average inventory levels. Further savings can be realized by having the goods classified as unassembled instead of assembled (tariffs can be as much as 50 percent lower on unassembled goods) and where wages are less than in the home country, assembly of products in an FTZ affords even more savings.

A similar alternative is the in-bond program (sometimes called *maquiladoras*) created in 1971 between Mexico and the United States. Through this program, the Mexican government allows U.S. processing, packaging, assembling, or repair plants located in the in-bond area to import parts and processed materials without paying import taxes, provided the finished goods are re-exported to the United States or to another foreign country. The United States, in turn, levies minimal tariffs on goods re-imported; the tariff is applied only on the value added while in Mexico. For many U.S. companies, this arrangement allows them to capitalize on lower Mexican wages ($1 to $2 per hour versus $4 to $6 or higher in the United States) to reduce overall product cost. This is especially important for products requiring substantial labor cost in production. Many U.S. manufacturers of lower-priced garments, for example, use in-bond arrangements. Most jeans manufacturers ship all the fabric parts for a pair of jeans to a *maquiladora* in Mexico for sewing, thus escaping much higher U.S. wage rates. Initially, most use of in-bond facilities were for goods re-imported for the American market. However, an increasing number of companies are utilizing this arrangement to lower costs of manufacturing for goods destined for export markets around the world. Over 400 U.S. companies producing clothing, toys, furniture, and electronics take advantage of this opportunity to lower production costs.[2]

Price Escalation: Summary

Price escalation is a fact of life for any firm attempting to market its products outside the home country. We have just reviewed how price escalation occurs and examined a number of possible strategies that the firm can use to reduce the landed price of the product. It is safe to say that most firms will employ whatever means at their disposal to keep the landed price of the product as low as possible.

Keep in mind, however, that the targeted final price at which the product is offered to the ultimate consumer is one element of the total international marketing mix. The final price of the product, as it stands in relation to the price of competitive products or to the price of available substitutes, is a function of the firm's international pricing goals and strategies; the nature of the product itself and its stage in the international product life cycle; the international promotional strategy used to introduce the product to the foreign market; and the distribution strategy used to deliver the product, all of which have been formulated as interactive parts in an overall strategic international marketing plan.

THE FIRM'S INTERNATIONAL PRICING OBJECTIVES AND GOALS

The objectives and goals of the international marketing operations of a firm are similar to those of the domestic operations—both operations expect to make a profit. In domestic marketing, typical pricing objectives include pricing for profit maximization, for return on investment (ROI), to increase total sales volume, or to increase market share. Similar objectives are set for international markets. One study surveyed U.S. and Canadian business firms, asking them to rate international pricing objectives on a scale from 1 (least important) to 5 (most important). Most important were profits, return on investments, market share, and total sales volume (all were rated between 4 and 5). Not surprisingly, liquidity received a low priority rating of 2.19.[3] In fact, as you might expect, because of the higher risks involved with marketing internationally, the company's executives will usually demand commensurately higher returns on whatever objective is set.

These pricing objectives guide the firm in developing subsequent pricing strategies and tactics and in setting the final price of the product. For example, if the company's pricing objective is to maximize short-term profits, the marketing department will set a price for the product that is as high as the market will bear, for as long as the market will bear it. If a specified return on investment is the goal, then the market will vary the elements of the marketing mix, including price, until the desired return on the investment is achieved. Promotional pricing tactics are indicated if an increase in total sales volume is desired, while setting a price below competitors' prices is the usual tactic designed to increase market share. The following sections discuss in more detail how these marketing principles are applied to international marketing situations.

THE PRODUCT LIFE CYCLE AND PRICING STRATEGIES

We introduced the concept of the product life cycle in Chapter 4 as an important marketing tool in developing product strategies. Here we will reintroduce the concept, this time as a useful guide for designing pricing strategy. As we discussed earlier, many products entering international markets, particularly from U.S. sources, will be in the introductory stage of their life cycle. To facilitate new product introduction, marketers generally employ one of three different pricing strategies; the choice of strategic framework is dictated by the stated pricing objectives of the firm, by the nature of the product itself, and by its stage in the product life cycle.

Skim-the-Cream Pricing Strategy

High technology products which are unique, have high research and development costs, are difficult for competitors to imitate, and which will appeal to innovators at a high introductory price use a *price skimming* or *skim-the-cream* pricing strategy. Skimming is a profit-oriented strategy where the price starts out high during the product's introduction to recoup as much R&D expense as possible, and of course to generate profit. Gradually, the firm must lower the price as imitative competitors enter the market. If you remember the pattern of pricing in the United States for calculators, microcomputers, or laser-disc players you were witnessing skim-the-cream pricing strategies.

In international markets, U.S. companies often follow such a skimming strategy. The unique nature of U.S. products, and (in some countries) the added prestige of the "made in America" label, enable U.S. firms to command a higher price for their products. Considering the high landed cost of most exports, this is fortunate for U.S. producers. However, the skimming strategy is no longer considered as ideal as it once was. One reason is that the "made in America" label has lost much of its intrinsic appeal in many markets. In addition, the accusation of "reverse dumping," or charging a *higher price* than the home market, is not unknown. The Canadian Royal commission called for direct action to reduce tractor prices in Canada when it was discovered that they were selling for 35 to 40 percent higher in Canada than in Britain.[4] Countries do not condone "profiteering" within their borders, particularly when the high-priced offender is the only supplier in the market.

Penetration Pricing Strategy

The alternative to a skim-the-cream pricing strategy is a *penetration* pricing strategy. With this approach, prices are very low at the outset to induce customers to try the product. Once a satisfactory level of market share is obtained, the firm raises it prices to improve profitability. This strategy is prominent with low-cost consumer products, such as health and beauty products, where product trial is important to adoption. It is also used to introduce products that are not easily differentiated, such as household cleaning products, where competitors can easily and quickly jump into the market with an imitative product if not discouraged by the low-priced introduction.

In recent years, the Japanese (as well as some other countries exporting to the United States) have been able to increase their share of the market partly through a penetration pricing strategy. This strategy has been helped by the strength of the U.S. dollar in comparison to the yen (and other currencies) throughout the early 1980s which served to further reduce the effective prices of foreign imports. The rebound of the yen in comparison to the dollar in 1986 may make a penetration pricing strategy more difficult in the future.

In addition, a penetration pricing strategy may prove to be a high-risk alternative if price competition forces the firm to sell the product below cost. Though "dumping" is defined differently by various economists, the most frequently used criteria are product prices that are lower than home country costs, or product prices that are lower than prices on comparable host country products. Companies that are accused of dumping goods in a market may face litigation and will be forced to raise prices by paying a "dumping surcharge." In 1986, for example, Japanese semiconductor manufacturers were forced to pay such a tax or penalty for dumping products at extremely low prices (below cost) on the U.S. semiconductor market. As another example, the Japanese share of the U.S. television market grew from 11 percent to 29 percent in a six-month period. U.S. manufacturers filed complaints about predatory pricing with the International Trade Commission of the U.S. Department of the Treasury accusing the Japanese of dumping television sets on U.S. markets. The Japanese manufacturers were required to implement across-the-board price increases. An increasingly important issue for pricing in international markets, dumping will be discussed in more detail later in this chapter.

Though objectives in international pricing may be stated in much the same terms as objectives for domestic markets, the strategies employed to implement those objectives will be greatly influenced by foreign uncontrollable market factors. Countries may object to prices above as well as below domestic prices. As a result, pricing to meet competition and emphasis on nonprice competition may be the most risk-averse approach.

Pricing to Meet Competition

The third alternative pricing strategy is usually used in domestic markets for undifferentiated products with an identifiable industry price leader. For example, in the steel industry, National Steel's stated objective is to follow the industry leader; similarly Goodyear Tire and Gulf Oil price their products to meet competitive price levels of firms in their respective industries. In addition, pricing to meet competition is used to move the competitive arena away from prices and to focus on other product attributes. Though price is an important part of the marketing mix, it is but one factor. Certainly prices must lie within a defined range intended to stimulate adequate market demands and to provide a profit to the firm. Prices should also be competitive in order for the product to succeed in the market. However for many products, especially industrial goods, price is a secondary consideration. Quality, uniformity, reliable delivery, and servicing may be the more important factors and, when provided effectively, will allow the product to support a higher price.

Most marketers, in fact, especially those in international markets, prefer to avoid price-based competition. Price-based competition reduces the profits of the companies involved and generally results in the success of only those large companies who can withstand the period of losses. The alternative, nonprice-based competition, focuses on product differentiation emphasized by strong promotional strategies to win customers. Messages touting product (or service) advantages which are geared to specific market segments are designed to carve a niche in the market. By promoting the product in this manner the firm hopes to maintain price integrity.

The Product Life Cycle and Pricing Strategies: Summary

International markets are comprised of people located outside the home country of the firm, with needs and wants and the means to satisfy those needs and wants. Total demand for the product is the net result of the combination of the following: (1) the "satisfaction value" of the product for the market; (2) the size of the market; (3) the market's ability to purchase. In some countries, for example, only a small part of the population may be able to afford a company's product at a profitable price while other countries will have large markets, with many firms competing for their share. When calculating the potential for the firm in that market, the availability of substitute products as well as the presence of competitors must be included in the demand equation. All this adds up to one basic rule of pricing: The firm must determine if sufficient demand will be generated at a price that will prove profitable.

We have seen that the firm's influence on pricing strategies coupled with market influences on pricing strategy create a complex environment for international pricing decisions. The marketer's pricing strategy is further challenged by regulations and laws imposed by host governments, which will be the focus of the next section.

COUNTERTRADE

This chapter has concentrated on the traditional approaches to pricing, where the marketer determines the appropriate amount of currency to be exchanged for the goods. Until recently a discussion limited to this traditional perspective may have been sufficient to provide an adequate overview of international pricing. Now, however, the astute international marketer must also become adept at countertrade in order to remain competitive.

More countries are demanding that companies accept goods or services instead of money for products they buy. Countertrade, or barter (one type of countertrade), is used for a variety of reasons. Soviet bloc countries frequently seek countertrades because they desire Western goods but lack the hard currency with which to purchase those goods on the market. Third World nations also desire Western goods, but cannot pay because of large debts to the West; they seek countertrades to be able to obtain the goods while keeping precious currency in the country.[5] In addition, these debtor countries may be required to restrict imports closely as a part of agreements made with lenders. Countertrade enables these countries to import goods without disrupting the balance of trade, since the imports would be matched by exports of relatively equal value.

Among the problems for the MNC in accepting countertrade is valuation of the merchandise received in a barter (What is the value of a shipload of Chinese straw hats?), the increased costs of handling countertrade transactions, and finding markets for resale of the goods received. Of course not all countertrades pose the problems the company accepting the straw hats would have. If a company can receive products it can use in a barter arrangement, the difficulties of countertrading are minimal. An example of a successful countertrade involves Pepsi-Cola's arrangement with the Soviet Union to trade Pepsi's soft drink syrup for Stolichnaya vodka; another is Pepsi's countertrade with Romania, where the soft drink syrup is traded for wine which is then marketed in the United States by a Pepsi-Cola company, Monsieur Henri Wines, under the "Premiat" label.

Most companies involved in countertrading are not as fortunate as Pepsi-Cola. McDonnell Douglas, the aircraft manufacturer, has received a wide range of products from Polish hams to Czechoslovakian crystal in trade for its DC-10s. In this case, for the company to have a profitable sale, it had to be able to place a value on the goods offered in trade in order to receive enough bartered goods to cover the desired price. The company then had to arrange to sell the hams and the crystal.

Knowledge of countertrading is an important part of an international marketer's pricing skills. If a customer offers to pay for a $500,000 order with $250,000 cash and $250,000 in sheep skins (an actual situation for Ford Motor Company in Peru), the marketer has got to know where to sell the sheep skins and how many it will take to generate the $250,000. These difficulties in valuation of goods and finding resale markets has led to the increased involvement of trading companies who have the global contacts and experience to handle such transactions.[6]

Both the issue of countertrade and the involvement of trading companies will increase in importance in the future. Marketers who expect to be competitive in international markets had best be familiar with these concepts. Chapter 8 deals specifically with future issues in international marketing and discusses both countertrade and trading companies in more depth.

GOVERNMENT INFLUENCES ON PRICING

Pricing may be one of the most heavily regulated areas in marketing, both domestically and internationally. The following section examines some of the major host-country influences on pricing.

Cartels

The Webb-Pomerene Export Trade Act of 1918 allows groups or cartels of U.S. firms called (WPEAs) to engage in international price setting, as long as the cartel does not affect U.S. domestic market competition. WPEAs have not been popular among U.S. businesses because of possible antitrust violations, since the determination of the effect of the WPEA on U.S. markets is not made until after the WPEA is in operation. The EC (European Community) generally approves export cartels as well, but discourages internal (within EC) collusion. World cartels exist in steel, glass, chemicals, and other industries. Most of you are probably familiar with the oil cartel: OPEC, the Organization of Petroleum Exporting Countries. OPEC, like many cartels, not only sets oil prices, but may attempt to control production and distribution to ensure that prices remain fixed. It is generally believed that cartels increase prices and reduce competition; and it is also agreed that they are very difficult to control.

Government Price Setting

In contrast to the "hands off" legislation discussed above, international marketers may also encounter government interference with prices. It is not uncommon for governments to regulate prices. Specified mark-ups, price freezes, price floors or ceilings, restrictions on price changes, and government subsidies are frequently encountered by the international marketer. For example, Argentina, Colombia, Brazil, and many other countries have all established temporary price freezes to help restrain inflation, as did the United States in 1971. Price ceilings are often imposed on staples such as bread, rice, and milk. Once price controls are imposed, governments are reluctant to eliminate them for fear of public outcry. Tunisia, for example, experienced food riots when price ceilings were lifted from bread and other basic foods. India and Spain require permission for price changes on a wide variety of products; even many cities in the United States regulate changes in rents and other prices.

The international firm may also encounter government monopolies that control all international selling or buying. Such is the case in Brazil where the IBC (Brazilian Coffee Institute) handles all international sales of raw coffee beans. On the buying end, the government may be the only customer for a firm's products. In East European countries, the Soviet Union, and in some cases the People's Republic of China, all purchases are made by government agencies regardless of whether the products are as seemingly insignificant as peanuts or as important as trucks. As you can imagine, having only one buyer does limit the negotiating room for a marketer.

In addition, tariffs and other government controlled barriers raise prices for selected goods. Tariffs of 200 to 300 percent are not unusual when a country desires to protect a developing industry by pricing imports out of the market. These prohibitive tariffs are seen in selected industries in countries such as Mexico, Brazil, and Argentina.

Dumping

One of the most controversial international business issues in the past decade has been dumping. The U.S. Congress defines dumping as "unfair trade practices—unfair price cutting having as its objective the injury, destruction, or prevention of the establishment of American industry." Under this broad definition, the United States considers a country to be dumping goods if the goods sell at prices lower than the prevailing home country price or lower than comparable U.S. goods. GATT (General Agreement on Tariffs and Trade) recognizes only the former; dumping occurs when goods are exported at lower than the normal domestic price.

In the United States, dumping proceedings have been on the rise. In one year the Treasury Department cited 23 out of 28 foreign automobile companies for dumping and forced price increases that resulted in a Volkswagen price increase of two and one half times over the prior year. Foreign firms exporting steel, television sets, shoes, and many other goods have faced dumping charges brought by U.S. industry. Most recently, the semiconductor industry in the United States has placed pressure on the U.S. government to investigate foreign firms, particularly from Japan, on charges of dumping semiconductors on the U.S. market at prices below cost.

Companies in the European Community have also voiced concern about dumping of photocopiers, semiconductors, and electronic components on European markets. The sales of Japanese compact-disc players, for example, quadrupled in less than one year despite a 19.5 percent EC tariff. EC competitors claim that the Japanese are not making any profit on the players, but are dumping them on the market. The Japanese deny charges of dumping goods, but cite favorable valuation of the yen vis-à-vis EC currencies.

Though lower prices might seem a boon to consumers in the short run, it is exactly the short-run nature of dumping to which economists object. When foreign producers flood the market with low-priced goods, consumers purchase the imports and neglect home country products. Domestic producers may be driven out of business because of losses sustained through price-cutting or through lost sales. The home country therefore loses a supply of that good, as well as losing jobs, tax revenues, and other benefits of the business.

There are a number of reasons that a firm might be tempted to dump goods onto a foreign market. The most obvious, as discussed earlier, is the desire to combat price escalation and to price products competitively. Though perhaps a sound marketing strategy, prices below cost may be considered dumping by the host country. However, there may be other reasons as well. Overproduction may create a need to move inventories. Storage space may be unavailable, or goods may be perishable. Rather than keep capital tied up, the company may desire the cash flow from selling inventory, even at a lower price. Communist countries are often in need of hard currency, and dump goods into the United States and Western Europe to obtain dollars, marks, pounds, or francs.[7]

One of the most complex issues in dumping is the determination of full manufacturer production costs, the basis of the dumping accusation. Many countries will not reveal production operating figures so that costs can be determined. To further complicate matters, the 1974 Trade Act (U.S.) forbids the use of production costs of a Communist country but uses instead comparable free-market figures. One of the most interesting cases under this act involved golf carts manufactured by Melex, a Polish aircraft company. A U.S. manufacturer claimed that Melex was dumping golf carts into U.S. markets. Melex raised its prices and paid duties based on a Canadian manufacturer's costs. When the Canadians stopped exporting golf carts, the U.S. Treasury Department constructed a "fair value" based on free-market countries with economic development approximating that of Poland. Spain and Mexico were selected. Unfortunately, neither makes golf carts, so costs were estimated *as if* golf carts were produced in those countries! The FTC then attacked this as *de facto* price setting, injurious to competition. The issue of dumping is obviously one of protecting home country industry. The Melex issue is a good example of the problems of establishing manufacturing costs. It also illustrates the lengths a country will go if there is a desire to prove dumping. Interestingly enough, the issue of dumping is seldom raised in industries with little political influence.

Antitrust Legislation

In the United States, the Sherman Antitrust Act of 1890 prohibits monopolies and other combinations in restraint of trade. This legislation was bolstered in 1914 with the passage of the Clayton Act which specifically addresses, among other things, price discrimination. You may recall that the Clayton Act amended the Sherman Antitrust Act by specifically prohibiting interlocking directorates, tying contracts, and collusive bidding. The 1936 Robinson–Patman Act deals even more specifically with price discrimination. These and other laws strictly regulate businesses in the United States.

Many other countries have antitrust legislation. West Germany is considered to have the toughest and most comprehensive antitrust laws outside the United States. The U.K. just passed a stiff Competition Bill which details seven areas of competition to be regulated, from supply restrictions of retailers to discriminatory pricing. Japan is revising and intensifying its antimonopoly laws, and the EC has been actively enforcing its antitrust laws since the 1970s. In one EC case, Michelin was fined $700,000 for operating a system of discriminatory rebates to Dutch tire dealers. Similar penalties have been assessed against the United Brand Company for price discrimination.

The MDCs are not the only countries that enact pricing legislation. Companies operating in LDCs must also be careful to remain within the host country's laws. While MDCs will legislate to protect trade between independent companies, LDCs are particularly concerned about parent company restrictions on LDC subsidiaries that may affect competition within their borders.

FINANCIAL CONSIDERATIONS

Besides government influences on price, there are financial considerations in international pricing, such as recovering payment at the expected value. The sale of goods in other countries is complicated by risks arising from problems of currency exchange and the cost and difficulty of collecting delinquent accounts should they occur. Two of the major issues are international commercial payments and exchange risks.

International Commercial Payments

Financial risks arise from inadequate customer credit reports, currency exchange controls, distance, different legal systems, and collection problems. In international transactions, payment is not as easy as writing a check. Ensuring that you will receive full payment once a sale is made can be a problem.

In U.S. domestic trade, established customers typically pay on an open account—the goods are delivered and the customer is billed on an end-of-the-month basis. However, the most frequently used type of payment in foreign commercial transactions is a letter of credit, followed closely in importance by bills of exchange. Open accounts are reserved for well-established customers.

How payment will be made is determined at the time of sale, and is considered part of the pricing arrangement. Three major payment methods are (1) cash in advance, (2) open accounts, and (3) letters of credit.

Cash in Advance. Because of the long lead time required in international trade, cash in advance is rarely required. It is unpopular with the customer, particularly when cost of capital is high, but is sometimes necessary when exchange restrictions may delay or prohibit payment, or when credit risk is high. More frequently, partial payment in advance is required. This is particularly the case when expensive machinery is made to customer specification, and losses due to an incomplete contract would be high.

Open Accounts. In international markets, open accounts are limited to customers of long standing with impeccable credit ratings. Open accounts place all the risk with the seller, including nonpayment risk and exchange risk. Though used commonly in domestic marketing, open accounts should be avoided internationally. The financial transaction most frequently used is the letter of credit.

Letters of Credit.   Export letters of credit are essentially a statement made to the seller by the buyer's bank that the buyer is "good for the money." Once the sales transaction is completed, the buyer goes to a local bank to arrange for issuance of the letter. When approved, the buyer's bank notifies its correspondent bank in the seller's country of the issuance of the buyer's letter of credit. Once the requirements set forth in the letter of credit are met (for example, completion of the terms of the sales contract), the seller can collect payment from the correspondent bank in the home country.

Once you receive payment your risk may still not be over. If you receive payment in a currency other than U.S. dollars and must exchange the foreign currency for U.S. dollars, you may lose money in the transaction. As we will discuss in the next section, currency values fluctuate in relation to one another. That is, these values are not permanent, but can change.

Currency Problems

Currency fluctuations add an additional economic uncontrollable variable. The valuation and exchange of currencies is an extremely complex subject. At this point it is important to understand that currencies change in relative value over time. You may have been reading about the "strong dollar." That means that the dollar was worth more than it had been in the past in relation to (for example) the Japanese yen, the French franc, or the British pound. As a result, in order to buy American products these countries had to spend more of their currencies to obtain dollars to make the purchase; this effectively raised the price of American exports. Reverse that situation and you will see why Japanese cars are so appealing to U.S. buyers: Dollars can buy more yen, so imported cars are effectively less expensive.

One of the important features about the value of money is that a country's currency can experience dramatic changes in value, relative to other nations' currencies, in just a short time. For example, in 1980 1 U.S. dollar bought 4 French francs, but by 1984 1 U.S. dollar bought 8.7 francs, a substantial decrease in the value of the French franc relative to the U.S. dollar. By 1986 the U.S. dollar had "weakened" somewhat, and 1 U.S. dollar bought 6.9 French francs. Changes in the value of the Mexican peso were even more dramatic. In 1980 1 U.S. dollar equaled 22 Mexican pesos, by 1986 that same dollar purchased over 600 pesos. In general, between 1980 and 1984, the value of the

U.S. dollar strengthened relative to most of the rest of the world's currencies; by mid-1986 the dollar had slowed its meteoric rise and began to weaken against other currencies, particularly against the Japanese yen and the West German mark. Today, when you are reading this, the dollar may be stronger or weaker than in 1986. Do Exercise 5–1 and see what has happened to the value of the dollar since 1980.

EXERCISE 5–1

Below is a list of relative values of several currencies to one U.S. dollar. Consult *The Wall Street Journal* or some other source and complete the table below. Has the value of the dollar, relative to the countries listed, gone up, down, or stayed the same since 1980? Explain the value of a nation's money changes.

Value of the Dollar in Four Countries

(One dollar bought:)*	1980†	1984	1986	Today
Mexico (peso)	22	193	633	_____
France (francs)	4	8.7	6.9	_____
Italy (lira)	800	1,746	1,473	_____
Japan (yen)	221	243	157	_____

*For example, one U.S. dollar bought 22 Mexican pesos in 1980.
†1980, 1984, and 1986 figures are July averages.

Exchange Risk

Exchange risk refers to the risk a firm assumes when it accepts one currency which it needs to convert to another in order to realize an expected profit. Because contracts are not consummated immediately and because there is a time span of months or years between the contract agreement, performance, and subsequent payment, the value of the currencies involved can change. Suppose you make a sale to a customer in France and they agree to pay you 5,000 French francs. At the time the sale was made the exchange rate was five francs per one U.S. dollar. Thus, you expected to receive the equivalent of $1,000 U.S. dollars for the sale. However, when you received the 5,000 francs and exchanged them for dollars, the exchange rate was 5.6 francs per dollar. At that exchange rate you will receive only $892, not the $1,000 you expected. Because of exchange risk you have had a $108 loss. Such currency fluctuations can severely affect profits, sometimes positively, sometimes negatively. Hewlett-Packard, for example, gained nearly half a million dollars through currency fluctuations in its favor; Nestle lost $1 million over six years due to unfavorable and uncontrollable currency fluctuations.[8]

Because of this uncertainty, companies doing business internationally utilize a number of techniques to offset exchange risks. They may write contracts denominated in a third country's currency (for example, U.S. dollars), so that both companies equally assume the risk of their respective currencies changing in relation to dollars. However, when there is a great deal of volatility in the value among nations' currencies, as has been true since the late 1970s, requiring contracts to be denominated in U.S. dollars may be unacceptable. The trend is for firms to use a variety of methods to diversify exchange risks.

A seller may agree to accept payment in a basket of currencies, thus diversifying exchange risk among several currencies. That is, a contract may be paid off with a combination of dollars, pounds, and marks. If the firm's home currency changes unfavorably with respect to one of the currencies in the basket, there is still a chance that it will be relatively favorable with respect to the other two. The seller may hedge against exchange risk by buying or selling offsetting contracts for future delivery of currencies. Finally, the selling firm may resort to the least acceptable alternative to the buyer by requiring payment in dollars and in advance. This may be done when exchange risk is very high, but often places the seller at a competitive disadvantage. Though a detailed examination of the various techniques used to offset the impact of currency fluctuations is well beyond the scope of this discussion, the following examples should provide an understanding of the basic concepts used by the international marketer to counter exchange risks.

Let us say that an English and a German firm sign a contract in pounds. The British will perform the contract and the Germans will pay in pounds in three months' time. If the mark loses relative value in that time, it will take more marks to buy pounds, and the contract will become more expensive for the Germans. If the Germans believe that the mark will be devalued, they may buy pounds at the time the contract is negotiated. Or, they may buy a forward contract for pounds to be delivered to them in three months' time. Alternately, England and Germany may both agree to write the contract in a basket of currencies, to diversify the risk. Germany would pay England, for example, one third of the contract price in dollars, one third in marks, and one third in pounds. That way both firms take on exchange risk. On the other hand, if the Germans believe that it is the pound that will be devalued, they will be happy to keep the contract in pounds. It will take fewer marks to buy pounds, effectively lowering the price of the contract.[9]

Because of their relative stability and liquidity, most U.S. international businesses prefer to write contracts in hard currencies, particularly the U.S. dollar. The effect of a strong currency forces high prices for its exports, and is an attractive market for imports. It can be advantageous when the country is in a debtor position, but disadvantageous when the strong currency firm is a creditor.

SUMMARY

Pricing is one of the more complex elements of the marketing mix. A multitude of variables must be considered in pricing planning, including product demand curves, competition, substitutes, pricing legislation, and financial considerations such as exchange risk and countertrades. Pricing strategy is considered a part of the controllable environment of the firm, yet as we have discussed here is greatly affected by both domestic and foreign uncontrollable elements.

NOTES

1. John Widdifield, "U.S. Businesses Are Still Neglecting to Take Advantage of Benefits of Foreign Trade Zones," *Marketing News,* December 23, 1983, p. 2.

2. "Mexico's In-Bond Industry Continues Its Dynamic Growth," *Business America,* November 26, 1984, pp. 26–28.

3. "Factors that Influence Pricing Decisions," *International Management,* June 1981, p. 3.

4. Ibid.

5. Richard N. Cooper, "Why Countertrade?" *Across the Board,* March 1984, pp. 36–42.

6. "Countertrade: Trade without Cash?" *Finance and Development,* December 1983, pp. 14–16.

7. Steven E. Plaut, "Why Dumping Is Good for U.S.," *Fortune,* May 5, 1980, p. 78.

8. Ihe Mathur, "Managing Foreign Exchange Risk Profitably," *Columbia Journal of World Business,* Winter 1982, pp. 22–30.

9. Laurent L. Jacque, "Management of Foreign Exchange Risk: A Review Article," *Journal of International Business Studies,* Spring–Summer 1981, pp. 81–101.

ADDITIONAL READINGS

Cateora, Philip R. *International Marketing.* Homewood, Ill.: Richard D. Irwin, 1987. See page 561 for an illustration of the effects of price escalation.

Cohan, Stephen S. and John Zysman. "Countertrade, Offsets, Barter, and Buybacks." *California Management Review,* Winter 1986, pp. 41–56.

Keegan, Warren. *International Marketing Management.* Englewood Cliffs, N.J.: Prentice-Hall, 1981.

CHAPTER SIX

International Distribution

Once a manufacturer has developed a product that the firm believes will satisfy the wants and needs of the target market (the focus of Chapter 4) and has determined a price at which the product will sell and the firm will make a profit (Chapter 5), the next marketing project is to map out the product's distribution strategy. U.S. manufacturers are accustomed to the availability of an extensive network of distribution channels which efficiently penetrate the domestic market. These distribution channels are comprised of a number of marketing institutions, which in combination, move goods from the producer to the consumer (or industrial user). A marketing distribution channel may include the following companies: (1) the actual channel members, or middlemen, such as wholesalers and retailers and (2) the institutions providing the necessary auxiliary services, such as transportation, warehousing, banking, or legal services. These channel members and the facilitating institutions are well established in the United States, and their operations are coordinated through a number of alternative channel structures from which the firm may choose. Accordingly, the degree of U.S. market penetration is unique. Whether the producer is trying to reach a small mountain town like Ouray, Colorado, or a major metropolitan area like New York City, an extensive distribution system is in place.

The U.S. firm entering international markets does not enjoy the same relative ease of distribution for the product as in the United States. First, the legal regulations are far more stringent and far more numerous. Permission from the home government must be obtained to export (or import) goods, and the host country must give permission for the goods to enter. Second, goods must be transported over greater distances and will most likely be transferred among a number of carriers. Third, once in the host country, the marketer may encounter difficulty in getting the product to the ultimate consumer. Each stage will require management decisions regarding such factors as physical transfer of goods, legal transfer of title, costs, timing, insurance, and financing. In short, the marketer cannot expect to find the same network of distribution channels found in the United States.

This chapter will address the differences involved when distributing goods internationally. The introduction suggests the most basic differences between distributing goods domestically and distributing them internationally: decreased availability of distribution channels and increased transportation, legal, and financial requirements. We will now examine the differences more carefully and look at the variety of options available in the international markets to accommodate these differences.

GETTING OUT OF THE UNITED STATES

The first step is to get the product out of the country. All governments control the movement of goods in and out of their countries; sometimes movement is restricted, other times it may be prohibited. This section looks at the U.S. requirements for export.

Licenses: Permission to Export

The U.S. government imposes certain restrictions on the export of goods. Most commodities, technical data, parts, and components are controlled by the Department of Commerce; the regulations are published in the *Export Administration Regulations*. Other products, such as weapons, atomic and fissionable goods, gold and silver, narcotics, natural gas, electric power, and endangered wildlife, are controlled by their respective federal agencies. The Department of Commerce also controls the re-export of commodities and technical data of U.S. origin from a foreign distributor to a third country, and of parts and components of U.S. origin which are used to manufacture foreign products for export.

Two types of licenses are issued: general and validated. A general license permits exportation within guidelines without requiring that an application be filed or a license document issued. A validated license authorizes exportation within specified limitations and is issued only upon formal application. The type of license issued depends upon two factors: country of destination and type of commodity. The Department of Commerce's *Country Groups Supplement* to the *Export Administration Regulations* and the *Commodity Control List* contain the necessary information.

The U.S. government classifies all countries of the world (with the exception of Canada) into eight groups (P, Q, S, T, V, W, Y, Z). The most stringent requirements are for Z group, which includes North Korea, Vietnam, and Cambodia. Validated licenses are required for almost all commodities destined for Z countries, if trade is permitted at all. It is important to note that the classification of a country may change over time, depending upon the diplomatic relations of the current administrations. China, for example, was once classified in Z group and little or no trade transpired. Today China is classified in a more favorable group where trade is not only permitted but is encouraged. Such changes in classification are often surrounded by political controversy, but it is the responsibility of the firm to be cognizant of current classifications as well as being aware of imminent changes.

Certain commodities will require a validated license regardless of destination. If so, validation must be obtained before any shipment is made. Furthermore, it is the responsibility of the exporter to take reasonable steps to ensure that the goods arrive at the destination declared on the license. Any attempts by the exporter to divert goods from the declared destination are illegal and can result in a prison term and/or fine. High technology products, such as computers and peripheral equipment, medical instruments, research and testing equipment, or other products that contain sophisticated electronic components, are likely to require validated licenses.

Once permission to export is obtained, the exporting firm must concern itself with the documentation required by its home country; the paperwork required by any commercial parties involved, such as financial and shipping institutions; and any documentation required by the host country.

Documentation

Documents for home country export, commercial payment, shipping, and host country import must accompany each export shipment. In fact, so many documents are required that many consider documentation the most frustrating of all nontariff trade barriers. A single shipment may require more than 50 documents and involve more than 28 different parties.[1] Regardless of the quantity of paperwork required, each document must be carefully completed. At the very least, errors will delay shipment. At worst, errors will be construed as deliberate attempts to defraud, and officials may impose penalties, fines, or may even confiscate shipments.

The most frequently required export documents include the following:

1. *Licenses*—validated or general, as discussed in the previous section.
2. *Export declaration*—required by the U.S. government as a control mechanism to determine quantity of goods leaving the country, their final destination, and to monitor compliance with regulations.
3. *Commercial invoice*—required for all international transactions by governments as well as financial institutions and carriers. It is a bill or statement of goods sold.
4. *Bill of lading*—required by legal and financial institutions as a certificate of title and by carriers as both a contract and a receipt between carriers and the shipper.
5. *Insurance policy*—usually required in the terms of sale by the financier or by the buyer. It is necessary due to the high risks involved in international transport.
6. *Consular invoice* or *Certificate of origin*—not always required; when it is, it must be painstakingly completed and usually involves a great deal of red tape.
7. *Special certificates*—includes health or sanitation certificates, inspection certificates for quality or safety, packing lists, or other documents required by the receiving country.[2]

GETTING TO THE HOST COUNTRY

In addition to getting permission to take the product out of the United States and compiling the documentation required to do so, the exporters must be concerned with shipping the product to the host country. First the product must be transported to the ultimate carrier. If the product is going by air, that may simply be a matter of getting to the nearest airport (probably by truck). If, however, the product is being transported by ship, it must get to the nearest port; that may involve both trucking and railroads. Once it reaches the host country, the product must then be transported internally to distributors and ultimate consumers. This section looks at some of the considerations involved in physically moving the product from the United States to the host country.

International Shipping

The most obvious differences in international physical distribution center around the greater distances involved. Goods are out of the control of the sender or buyer for longer periods of time; for example, it may take months to get from the United States to India via ship.

Changes in the product's physical environment may be drastic, requiring protective or environmentally controlled containers (think about a product moving from the cold climate of Canada to countries in the tropics). More transfers are necessary between carriers, providing opportunity for damage, theft, or other losses at each point. More insurance will be required, and more documents will be required to satisfy the requirements of each new transaction.

For U.S. exporters, options for transporting goods are limited to air freight or ocean shipping, with the exception of shipments to Canada and Mexico which can also be transported by railroad and by truck. Ocean shipping is usually the least expensive method for transoceanic shipments, especially for bulky, heavy goods with no time constraints on delivery. Though ocean shipping has its critics regarding the efficiency and reliability of its operations, the advent of containerization has improved the safety and efficiency of both ocean and rail shipping. Air freight is used for goods of high value, low weight and volume, or with time constraints. For example, newspapers, magazines, books, and periodicals; industrial machinery, electrical machinery, and agricultural machinery; drugs, chemicals, and pharmaceuticals; and clothing and textile products often move by air freight.

The physical carrier decision is best made on a total marketing basis. For example, air freight has the highest up-front cost. But shipping by air saves time; if the product has a high unit value, high inventory cost, or if the sale depends on fast delivery, then the cost may be justified. In addition, air freight may have lower packing requirements, lower insurance rates, and less damage.

Protection and Identification. Goods destined for international markets must be carefully packed. They may require crating against rough handling; protection against heat, moisture, or temperature extremes; and containers that discourage pilferage. Care must be taken to mark goods and containers exactly as regulations specify. The Department of Commerce publishes *Preparing Shipment to (Country)*, which details exact regulations regarding documents, labels, marking, packing, and customs procedures.[3]

The mechanics of exporting as described above are unique to exporting and require painstaking attention to detail. Errors, omissions, and negligence can lead to long delays and increase costs. Even "innocent" errors have unfortunate results. One New York firm exported carefully packed goods to an Arab nation, only to have the shipment confiscated upon arrival. The firm had unwittingly protected the merchandise with newspapers—written in Hebrew. Most Arab nations do not recognize Israel and boycott all companies doing business with Israel.

GETTING INTO THE HOST COUNTRY

Once the products leave the home country and are transported to the borders of the host country, permission must be obtained for the goods to enter. In previous chapters we have examined, in some detail, the factors that influence host country entry requirements. Here we will briefly review the nature of these possible barriers to entry and the changes in the marketing mix that might be required to overcome these barriers, allowing the product to cross the border into the host country.

Legal barriers could require changes in the physical product, including packaging, labeling, materials, quality standards, instructions, or changes in almost any other element of the extended product (as discussed in Chapters 2 and 4). *Tariffs* and other *nontariff barriers* including quotas and customs fees must be paid (Chapter 2). *Import licenses* may be required, as might *currency permits* to allow payment. *Special certificates,* especially regarding health and sanitation concerns or for potentially harmful products, may be required. *Overseas Business Reports (OBRs)* of the Department of Commerce provide the international marketer with current information about these regulations.

INTERNATIONAL MIDDLEMEN

The question of who will handle export mechanics requires a rather substantial analysis of a wide variety of options. Large, experienced global marketing companies may have entire export departments, in-house, that coordinate and execute the export documentation, transportation, and physical distribution details. Most firms, however, rely on the use of middlemen for all or part of the international distribution of the product. Some of these middlemen are unique to international marketing and will be discussed in some depth in the next sections. Other middlemen function in a manner parallel to domestic middlemen and will be reviewed in the sections immediately following.

Middlemen Unique to International Markets

International middlemen operate under a variety of names and perform any number of functions. Inexperienced marketers seeking substantial assistance with international distribution most frequently use foreign freight forwarders, export management companies, or export trading companies, which offer the full range of services. These middlemen generally start with a basic package of services that the client must buy, then add on services as desired by the client (the manufacturer). In addition, some of the larger domestic manufacturers who have considerable experience in overseas markets and who maintain in-house export divisions may take on other noncompeting products in what is known as "piggybacking" or "complementary marketing" arrangements. This section will explore these options.

Foreign Freight Forwarders. These are, for many firms, indispensable international agents who are expert in handling the details of export shipments. Their services range from relatively simple services, such as handling physical distribution logistics, to the handling of all aspects of documenting and executing overseas distribution. A foreign freight forwarder can assume the entire task of getting the product on its way to the host country. Manufacturers may select among the following services:

Consulting.
Transportation counseling including shipping rates and scheduling, storage, containerization, packing, marking, transfers, and so on.
Legal counseling including product standards, labeling requirements, packaging, sizing, ingredients or component regulations.
Documentation including licenses, permits, invoices, bills of lading, and so on.
Insurance.
Financing.
Warehousing.

Because foreign freight forwarders are considered experts in the physical distribution area, even international middlemen or manufacturers who handle other aspects of the distribution function in-house may employ foreign freight forwarders to take over these specialized distribution functions.[4]

Trading Companies. These are international businesses that buy, sell, accumulate, transport, and distribute goods among many different companies representing a wide variety of countries. Though the Japanese trading companies may be the most well known to U.S. consumers today, trading companies hail from a number of different countries including the United States. In fact, the trading company concept is centuries old. You have probably read about the Hudson's Bay Company and the East India Company which prospered during the 16th, 17th, and 18th centuries. These companies would take a variety of manufactured goods from Europe to trade in the Far East for natural resources such as teas or silks. Besides performing the physical functions of transporting merchandise and negotiating trades, the trading companies provided another important function: They solved the problems of bilateral trade by coordinating transactions between a number of buyers and sellers.

Today's trading companies, such as Japan's Mitsubishi or the Soviet Union's Amtorg, operate on much the same concept. Some trading companies were designed for export, while others were originally designed for import. Of the import-oriented group, the best examples are the Japanese trading companies (*sogo shosha*). Contrary to what most Americans might think, those companies actually import more goods into Japan from the United States than they export from Japan to the United States. Any firm that attempts to sell its products in Japan would be wise to do so through one of their many trading companies, which will provide the contacts necessary to successfully penetrate the market. There are presently some 300 Japanese trading companies doing $240 billion in business annually; the two largest are Mitsubishi and Mitsui.[5]

In addition to being involved in importing and exporting, these trading companies offer auxiliary services such as financing, development of joint ventures, technical assistance, and even production of goods. Because of their global contacts the Japanese trading companies are also becoming well-known intermediaries. These "Third Nation" or "offshore" deals match two foreign countries, a country and a foreign company, or two foreign companies for their mutual benefit. For example, Nissho-Irvai Corporation arranges for Nike shoes (Oregon, U.S.A.) to be manufactured in South Korea and Taiwan and then sold in the United States and other countries throughout the world.

In previous chapters we have referred to the U.S. export trading companies (ETCs), a similar type of trading company to the ones just discussed, but one with some unique features. The U.S. export trading company is a product of the Export Trading Company Act of 1982 which was designed to encourage the formation of American-based export trading companies. To date about 45 applications have been processed for U.S. ETCs; though the legislation was passed to facilitate American business entry into global markets, many ETCs are finding that U.S. businesses are still hesitant to market their products internationally.[6] Chapter 8 provides an in-depth discussion of both the provisions of the Export Trading Company Act of 1982 and of global export trading companies currently in operation.

Export Management Companies.   *EMCs* are international middlemen who are able to handle all aspects of exporting and marketing overseas for the U.S. firm. They are well suited for companies whose international sales volume is small, who are inexperienced with foreign markets in general or with a specific foreign market, or who do not want to become immediately involved with the complexities of international marketing. EMCs are able to operate both under their own letterhead as export distributors, taking title to the goods before selling abroad; or they may sign an exclusive contract to represent a client in a particular foreign market operating under the manufacturer's letterhead. In this latter arrangement, EMCs may work so closely with a manufacturer as the firm's marketing department that customers may not realize that the EMC is an independent firm.

EMCs generally specialize by product categories, which allows them to perform extensive market services with a small professional staff. They may prepare advertising and promotional materials and recommend product changes; they make use of their overseas market contacts to facilitate marketing efforts; and their foreign language proficiency enables them to communicate effectively for their clients. They provide financial consulting, assist with obtaining financing, and may in fact assume credit risks. EMCs also perform market research, handle government regulations and documentation, consolidate shipments, and provide legal counseling. Some handle imports, and a few deal in countertrades though on a limited basis. For these services, the contracting firm will pay a retainer fee to the EMC, as well as a percent of sales, which may vary from 10 to 20 percent, depending on services performed.

One disadvantage of EMCs is that market penetration may not be as extensive as desired. Since the EMC generally works on the aforementioned commission basis it is dependent on sales volume for its revenues. EMCs may therefore limit market entry to high-volume markets, neglecting the development of smaller markets that are slower to catch on.

Generally speaking, EMCs differ from export trading companies (ETCs) in the scope of their business operation and in the diversity of their product lines. While EMCs are generally limited to functioning as the export sales department of a firm, ETCs additionally handle import trade and trade between foreign countries. However, under the conditions for the Export Trading Act of 1982, we may see some EMCs evolve into ETCs.[7]

Complementary Marketing or Piggybacking.   This service is offered by some large U.S. firms that have established distribution channels overseas. These firms may take on noncompeting products to fill out their own product lines or to even out seasonal distribution schedules. By offering more extensive product lines, the manufacturer may achieve greater economies of scale in distribution as well as provide more of an inducement for a distributor to take on the line. For example, General Electric Company has been distributing the merchandise of other companies through its international channels for over 50 years.

Singer Sewing Machine piggybacks complementary goods such as fabrics, patterns, and notions; Sony piggybacks Whirlpool appliances in Japan; and Schick distributes the Breck line of shampoo and hair products in Germany for American Cyanamid. The advantages to piggybacking include the established distribution channels and the shared fixed costs of exporting. Disadvantages include the lack of control over the product once it leaves the manufacturer and the problems associated with trying to service or support warranties on a product when it is distributed by another company.

Middlemen Linking Foreign Markets[*]

In addition to the type of international middlemen discussed above, there are others found both in the home country and in host countries that are important in international distribution. Many are very similar to the agent and merchant middlemen found in U.S. markets. These types of middlemen (here called exporters) specialize in representing U.S. firms in overseas markets. Similarly, agent and merchant middlemen in other countries specialize in representing overseas foreign manufacturers in the middleman's home market. Though some of the titles of international middlemen are the same as domestic middlemen, the marketer cannot assume that the functions, services, quality of service, reputation, or fees are also the same. Each middleman must be carefully researched before the firm makes a commitment to allow the middleman to take a product abroad or to engage a foreign country middleman as a representative.

Middlemen Located in the Home Country

Among the advantages of using domestic exporters is that they will be geographically closer to the firm, will speak the same language, and will utilize the same legal (and therefore contractual) system. For these reasons they may be more convenient for the U.S. firm to use. However, a major disadvantage of domestic exporters is that they are far removed from their prospective markets and as such may not provide as current, accurate, and perceptive information as their foreign counterparts.

Domestic Export Agents. As you may recall from our earlier discussion, export agents located in the home country generally work on

---

[*]For a description of other types not discussed fully in this section see Appendix B.

a commission basis and by definition do not take title to the merchandise. Besides the EMCs and WPEAs previously discussed, which provide extensive services, other more limited domestic export agents including manufacturer's export agents and buying offices are available.

Domestic Export Merchants.   The other type of middleman located in the home country is the domestic export merchant, who buys and sells merchandise on its own account. This is a good source of distribution for a firm that does not wish to become deeply involved in international marketing. As far as the manufacturer is concerned these middlemen are effectively the end of the distribution channel since the manufacturer often has little or no control in the marketing of the product beyond that point. Merchant middlemen are a low-cost channel for the manufacturer: They take over all risk with the title and are relatively easy to contact. Domestic export merchants may also operate as export jobbers who buy damaged merchandise, or export buyers who are hired by the buyer to find merchandise.

Middlemen Located in the Host Country

Because they are located in the host country, foreign middlemen have the advantage of being closer to the market, but the disadvantage of being more difficult for the manufacturer to contact and control. Carefully chosen foreign middlemen may allow the manufacturer to maintain more control over the product's distribution in the international market than their domestic counterparts. However, as with the domestic middlemen, degree of control depends on the type of middleman selected. The two major types discussed here are the foreign agent middlemen and the foreign merchant middlemen.

Foreign Agent Middlemen.   As with domestic export agents, foreign agent middlemen operate under a variety of names but have it in common that none takes title to the products. Some of their names are similar to the names of domestic agents (manufacturer's representatives, brokers, factors, and managing agents) and in fact many operate in a similar fashion with the only difference being their host country location. However, the firm cannot assume that the services performed will be the same, so negotiations must clearly specify the responsibilities and duties of each party.

Foreign Merchant Middlemen.   Again, like domestic merchant middlemen, foreign merchant middlemen take title to, and usually possession of, the goods. The names of the foreign merchants correctly imply that their function is very similar to their domestic counterparts:

distributors, dealers, jobbers, wholesalers, and retailers. Merchant middlemen offer the least involvement for the firm, since they handle their own credit, financing, shipping, storage, insurance, pricing, and promotion. For the same reasons, they also provide the manufacturer with the least amount of control. They will promote products in their own interest; that is, established, high-margin, high-turnover products.[8]

As we shall see in the following sections, the major difference here may be in the scope of business of these middlemen, and consequently in the number of middlemen that the exporting firm must contact (the latter is almost always greater). As we have observed, coverage of the markets, costs and margins, services performed, level of marketing expertise and involvement, and control of the product by the manufacturer will all vary greatly.

INTERNATIONAL RETAILING MIDDLEMEN

Our discussion until now has centered largely on middlemen who facilitate export transactions and on wholesaling middlemen (middlemen selling to other middlemen, such as retailers, or to industrial users). In this section we will concentrate on those institutions selling to the ultimate consumer.

International retailing middlemen are characterized by greater diversity than other international middlemen. Differences in intensity of distribution, breadth and depth of product lines, ownership patterns, pricing patterns, services offered, operations, and social acceptance are all cause for rethinking the retail sector of the distribution strategy when entering each new foreign market.

Review: U.S. Retailing

As a quick review, let us look at U.S. retailing in terms of those criteria mentioned above. The United States has an intense network of distribution channels; there are approximately 1.9 million retailers in the United States.[9] This number includes not only isolated stores, but stores located in unplanned shopping areas such as downtown business districts and in planned shopping centers such as neighborhood centers and community centers. Regional shopping malls join as many as 200 to 300 stores under one roof, ranging from small specialty stores like The Gap (selling jeans) or B. Dalton's (books), to large department stores like Sears or Montgomery Ward (selling everything from dishwashers to socks). Most of these nearly 2 million retailers are small independent shops; the others are huge chain stores with literally hundreds of branch stores located all over the United States.

The United States also supports retailers with a variety of pricing structures and levels of customer service. Top quality, exclusive merchandisers like Neiman-Marcus command high margins but pamper their "clients." Equally successful in entirely different markets are the discounters such as K mart and Wal-Mart, with no frills and low margins. In addition to in-store retailing, consumers can purchase goods from vending machines, catalogues, door-to-door salespeople, television or telephone sales, and even computers (called videotex). U.S. retailing is unique in the world in terms of variety of merchandise, services, types of stores, form of ownership, and intensity of distribution.

Comparison: U.S. and International Retailing

Intensity.   As we have mentioned, the international retailing situation is quite different from that in the United States. For example, international market penetration will rarely be as deep as in the United States; most countries' distribution systems are less intensive. When first entering an international market this may not present a problem, since introductory channel strategy often calls for exclusive or selective distribution. However, the situation changes as the market matures, when more intensive distribution is desired but may be difficult or impossible to obtain. In addition, though distribution in major urban areas may be similar throughout the world, many countries have population concentrations that are 50 percent or less urbanized. Reaching those rural markets can be extremely difficult and requires reaching hundreds of small retailers.

Breadth and Depth of Product Lines.   Some countries, like Italy and Morocco, favor many narrow line retailers; others, like Finland, prefer general merchandise retailers with very broad lines. Europe in recent years seems to have become a retailing paradox. Many European countries, particularly France and Germany, are characterized by numerous small, single-line shops. For example, to buy bread, sausage, fish, and canned peaches in France, one might visit the *patisserie* (for bread), *charcuterie* (for deli meats), *poissonerie* (for seafood), and *epicerie* (for groceries). Alternately, one might visit the French *hypermarché* or German *verbrauchmarkt* which are huge warehouse-type retailers stocking all of the above, plus clothing, beauty aids, automotive parts, household products, and a myriad of other goods. The marketer seeking entry into European or other markets must not rely on his SRC but must investigate all available options in the host country. Retailing is changing in many countries, like France and Germany, and the marketer should keep abreast of current trends.[10]

Pricing.   Markups and retailer margins are also changing. Discounting is becoming a major global trend, especially in more developed nations. National and international brand awareness and increases in advertising, coupled with general international support of price competition, have paved the way for the discounters. In Germany, for example, discount retailers first opened in 1953. Ten years later there were more than 300, and by the 1980s there were well over 2,000 discounters operating in Germany. Even though retail pricing is changing in many countries, the majority of goods sold throughout the world are sold by small retailers at prices that reflect high retail margins.

Ownership Patterns.   Economic development often reveals the need for shorter, more efficient market channels; as a result, many of these more developed countries are experiencing an increase in vertical integration of distribution channels. Though few yet equal the integrated channel systems of the United States which include corporate-owned chains, administered (power-directed) channels, franchises, or wholesaler-directed cooperative groups, the channels of distribution in many countries are changing in that direction. For example, by 1978 well over 30 percent of the grocery stores in the U.K. were chains, superstores, and supermarkets, a change from the Mom and Pop retailers that had prevailed prior to the 1960s. Self-service stores are also on the rise. Starting in the United States in the 1930s, only Sweden and Germany followed the lead in self-service supermarkets (around 1938). After World War II, however, the self-service trend in Europe increased, accompanied by a significant reduction in retail salesforces. Other parts of the world have not followed so quickly; Korea, for example, saw its first supermarket open in 1971.

Other ownership patterns, less familiar to the United States, abound. Many countries have combination wholesaler-retailers: Retailers who make sales to other middlemen as well as to the ultimate consumer. Consumer cooperatives are much more popular in Europe than in the United States; in Switzerland, co-ops account for one fifth of retail food stores and over one fourth of retail food sales. In Scandinavia, leased space co-op department stores are popular.

Services.   The firm moving into foreign markets must be specific regarding the kinds of services offered by international middlemen. Credit, selling support, displays, and other services offered by domestic middlemen may be unavailable overseas. Stocks and inventories in many countries are often maintained at levels below U.S. manufacturers' expectations, and in fact stores often "stock out" because of the high cost of capital and other inventory-related carrying costs. As we have mentioned previously, middlemen overseas are generally unfamiliar with test marketing or other types of marketing research as well, so the U.S. firm may encounter setbacks when attempting to perform these marketing functions.

As a result, more of these responsibilities must be handled by the manufacturers. For example, a middleman may decide to operate with only small shipments in order to keep inventories low. Such operations will then leave the manufacturer holding inventory, along with the cost of insurance, cost of capital, and other associated carrying costs. The manufacturer may also decide to support a program designed to induce middlemen to become more involved with the sale of the product. While this is not impossible to achieve, the manufacturer cannot always expect the same level of cooperation or degree of sophistication from foreign retailers regarding point-of-purchase displays, market research, in-store promotions, and other U.S. marketing tools as is standard operating procedure at home. The accumulation of these additional responsibilities can and will add greatly to the manufacturer's overall cost of distributing the product.

Nonstore Retailing.   As in the United States, nonstore retailing is increasing globally. U.S. direct marketing sales topped $110 billion in the 1980s and sales are increasing all over the world. Annual direct marketing sales average $10 billion in West Germany; $3 billion in France and the U.K.; and $2.4 billion in Japan. One successful international direct marketer, Avon, has an Asian sales force of 10,000 generating door-to-door sales in excess of $200 million.

Computer selling was adopted in many countries several years before it was introduced to the United States. Videotex is a computerized direct marketing system whereby the user can obtain information on a wide variety of products via a computer terminal and order merchandise at the same time. The U.K. was the first to adopt videotex in 1978; their system is known as "Prestel." Other early adopters were Japan (in 1979 with "Captain"); Finland (in 1979 with "Teleset"); and Sweden (in 1980 with "DataVision"). West Germany, Canada, Holland, and France also have videotex available in certain areas. These computerized retailing systems should still be considered experimental.[11]

Multinational Retailers

We have been discussing international retailing from the perspective of the manufacturer in the home country seeking a retail outlet in the host country through which the product can be distributed to the ultimate consumer. At this point we will take time to briefly discuss some retailers who operate on an international level.

One growing development has been the export of U.S. retail operations overseas. Though Sears and F. W. Woolworth may be considered the "old timers" of international retailing, some newer U.S.-based retailers have recently ventured overseas. K mart, Safeway, Target, and J. C. Penney stores, to name a few, operate in countries throughout the world. In addition, fast food franchisers such as Dairy Queen, Burger King, McDonald's, Pizza Hut, and Kentucky Fried Chicken have found profitable markets worldwide. McDonald's, for example, operates 1,085 fast food restaurants in 30 countries as well as its 442 outlets in Canada (in addition to the 6,251 locations in the United States); Burger King operates in 12 countries including Australia, the Bahamas, Canada, Denmark, England, Guam, Puerto Rico, France, Spain, Sweden, Hong Kong, and West Germany.

In turn, foreign retailers have begun invading U.S. borders. Bennetton, an Italian-based chain of high fashion knitwear, is sprouting branches all over the United States. Laura Ashley (U.K.) stores have been well received in the United States, particularly after the firm moved the stores to mall locations and away from the small hideaway locations that characterize their presence in Europe. In addition to the small specialty store chains, some large-scale retailers are entering U.S. markets as well. Ikea, a Swedish-owned furniture "megaretailer," has opened a store outside Philadelphia and plans another outside Washington D.C. Ikea started in Sweden as a wood-product company and evolved into a furniture manufacturer. Gradually the firm became a large-scale furniture retailer with stores throughout Europe.

The French have opened a Biggs hypermarket in Cincinnati, Ohio. The store has 40 checkout lanes, 75 aisles, carries 60,000 items, and employs 800 people to keep the behemoth store, which is one and one half times the length of a football field, in operation. Opened in October 1985, Biggs has averaged 50,000 shoppers a week, more than five times the average supermarket, with annual revenues in excess of $100 million.

The success of these international retailers suggests that marketers can expect to see more importing and exporting of middlemen operations, providing yet another avenue for the global distribution of products and services. The final section of this chapter discusses the last link in the distribution chain: coordinating the services of the various middlemen into one continuous marketing channel of distribution.

INTERNATIONAL CHANNEL STRATEGY

In domestic markets, channel composition and coordination, including channel length and degree of market penetration, are marketing tools in the control of the firm. The extensive, well-established nature of

U.S. distribution channels provides the marketer with these options. Because of this, distribution can be fully utilized as an element of marketing planning in domestic markets.

Channel strategy is quite different when moving a product from a domestic producer to an international customer. The first thing the marketer should realize is that the firm will probably lose control of the product before it reaches the final customer. That is, for the U.S. firm going into international markets the objective may be to get the product into the hands of a reputable middleman, who will then be responsible for getting the product to the international customer. When this happens, the channel of distribution cannot be utilized as a marketing tool to the same degree as in domestic marketing.

Part of the reason is channel coordination. Whether channel power is contractual, administered, or corporate, most U.S. distribution channels are coordinated to work toward achieving mutual goals. Whether "channel captain" is the manufacturer or the retailer, the channel members view channel strategy as part of an overall plan that, if well executed, will benefit all. This coordination is not often present in international distribution. In other countries middlemen operate much more independently. They do not see themselves as a link between the U.S. producer and the foreign consumer but as separate and independent entities.

Another key difference in international distribution is availability of middlemen. As we noted earlier, the widespread network of distributors that effectively and efficiently penetrates the U.S. market is unavailable in most international markets. In the MDCs, distribution channels penetrate much of the market, but they may not be as coordinated or efficient as U.S. channels. In LDCs, market penetration is greatly reduced because of the absence of an efficient distribution network. Though major urban areas the world over may enjoy comparable distribution channels, rural areas, particularly in LDCs, may be very difficult to reach. This shortage of available middlemen reduces the effectiveness of channel strategy in two ways: (1) market penetration is often greatly reduced, and (2) marketers select channel members not on the basis of cooperativeness or performance, but simply because they are available.

A fourth difference is channel length. International distribution channels tend to be much longer than domestic channels for the same goods. The reason is not only that greater distances must be traversed, but also because of the composition of the channel. International channels are often composed of many, smaller middlemen who offer much more limited services than found in the U.S. market.

Smaller middlemen may not be prepared to offer either complete warehousing operations or financing, services that are traditionally offered by U.S. middlemen. As a result, the phenomenon of spreading

---

Exhibit 6–1

The International Distribution Process:

Getting Out of the U.S.	Getting to the Host Country	Getting into the Host Country
Licenses	International	Tariffs, taxes
General	shipping and	Nontariff barriers
Validated	logistics	Standards
Documentation	Packing and	Inspection
Export declaration	protecting	Documentation
Commercial		Quotas
invoice		Fees
Bill of lading		Licenses
Insurance policy		Special
Consular invoice		certificates
Special		
certificates		

---

distribution costs among a number of middlemen which occurs in the efficient U.S. channels is absent in many international channels. In this case the costs of warehousing and financing inventory are pushed back to the manufacturer, as international middlemen will only order as much as they can sell in a relatively short time span (inventory measured in days or weeks compared to weeks or months in the United States.) Multiply this by the numerous channels required to achieve even adequate market penetration and you can see how manufacturer's distribution costs begin to multiply. In this way, inefficient global channels of distribution contribute to price escalation.

SUMMARY

This may seem a rather extensive overview of the international distribution process. However, it really only scratches the surface of what is a very complex subject. The outline in Exhibit 6–1 is designed to help your review and to organize in your own mind all of the topics discussed in this chapter. Appendix B, at the end of the text, provides a more detailed glossary of the numerous international distribution institutions.

To review, we first examined home country requirements for moving goods in or out of the country. Next, we discussed some of the key issues in transporting goods to the international destination and reviewed the entry requirements of the host country. Following an over-

---

Exhibit 6–1 *(concluded)*

The International Distribution Players:

Domestic Middlemen	Middlemen Unique to International Marketing	Foreign Middlemen
Merchants	Foreign freight	Merchants
Export merchants	forwarders	Distributors
Export jobbers	Export trading	Dealers
Export buyers	companies	Import jobbers
Foreign importers	Complementary	Wholesalers
Agents	marketers	Retailers
Manufacturer's		Agents
export agents		Manufacturer's
Brokers		representatives
Selling groups/		Brokers
WPEAs		Factors
Buying offices		Managing agents

---

view of the process, particular institutions which are in business to facilitate international trade were defined; additional types of middlemen are listed and defined in Appendix B. Finally, we analyzed the impact that the unique international distribution systems would have on channel strategy and on price escalation.

EXERCISE 6–1

You represent a major manufacturer of personal computers. You have not previously sold products in other countries but are now interested in selling your computers in Germany. The final users of your product in the United States are individual consumers for private and personal use and business customers. You expect to sell your computer to the same types of consumers in Germany. As you know, there are several alternatives for distribution. For each of the situations (*a* and *b* below), draw a flow chart of the path the product will take to reach the final user (both personal users and business users). List, by name, each middleman that will be used (1) to get the product out of the United States, (2) to get the product to the host country, and (3) to get the product to the final user.

   a. You want to sell to or have represent you, middlemen located in your home country.

   b. You want to sell to or have represent you, middlemen located in the host country.

NOTES

1. Marta Ortiz Buonafina, *Profitable Export Marketing* (Englewood Cliffs, N.J.: Prentice-Hall, 1984), Ch. 8.

2. Ibid.

3. *A Basic Guide to Exporting,* U.S. Department of Commerce, November 1981.

4. "Freight Forwarders: The Export Experts," *Distribution,* March 1980, pp. 37–40.

5. "Can Japanese Trading Companies Do Battle for U.S. Manufacturers?" *American Import/Export Management,* June 1984, pp. 18–22.

6. "K mart Is Peddling Its Knowhow in the Third World," *Business Week,* August 22, 1983, pp. 45–48.

7. "Export Management Companies—Your Outside Export Office," *American Import/Export Management,* May 1984, pp. 48–52.

8. "Exporters Wrestle with Market and Distribution Selection Problems in Penetrating New Markets," *Marketing News,* December 23, 1983, p. 10.

9. Jerome McCarthy, *Basic Marketing* (Homewood, Ill.: Richard D. Irwin, 1982), p. 406.

10. "Convenience Stores: The Fastest Growing Retailers," *Focus Japan,* January 1983, pp. 3–4.

11. "What's New in International Retailing?" *World,* published by Peat Marwick (accounting firm), April 1983, p. 25.

CHAPTER SEVEN

International Promotional Strategy

No matter how carefully or creatively a product has been designed, it will never satisfy wants and needs if the consumer is unaware of it. The objective of a good promotional strategy is to inform the consumer about the product and to persuade the consumer to buy. The promotional campaign must communicate the availability and value of the product to the target market, utilizing an effective combination of the elements of the promotional mix.

This chapter examines promotional strategy in an international context. We will look first at the application of the communications process model to international marketing, and then examine in detail issues relevant to the key components of the model. We will then discuss each element of the promotional mix vis-à-vis the differences caused by entering international markets. As in previous chapters, keep in mind that we are adapting domestic marketing principles to international situations.

COMMUNICATIONS PROCESS

The goal of marketing communications is to relay a message from a sender (the marketer) to a receiver (the consumer) intact. That is, information about a product—its availability, value, attributes, advantages, and so forth—must pass from the marketer to the consumer without being changed or distorted. The communications process model is a useful tool for analyzing how that goal might be achieved.

EXHIBIT 7–1

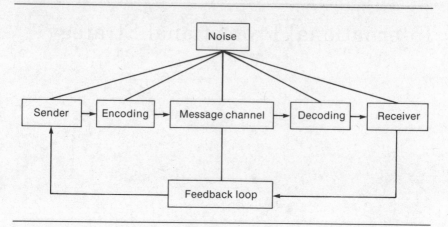

The process involves seven components, including the sender and the receiver. An error or miscommunication could be caused by mis-specifying any one of, or a combination of, those components. Breaking the communication process into stages aids the marketer in anticipating or identifying more accurately where a communication may be altered or lost. Exhibit 7–1 outlines the communications process. From your study of marketing, you are probably already familiar with this model. Even if you are not familiar with it, this section will explain briefly some key points about each component. The emphasis will of course be from the perspective of each component's application to international marketing communications.

Sender

By this time all other elements of the marketing mix are in place, decisions have been made regarding the product, its price, and its distribution. The sender (i.e., the marketer) must communicate this information to the target market, in this case an international market. More importantly, the marketer must communicate to the foreign market the crucial message: "this product satisfies your want or need." To do so, the marketer must correctly identify the need and explain how this product will satisfy that need. If the sender (marketer) makes an error in devising that message, the prospective foreign consumer may perceive no reason to buy the product.

Here again, the marketer's SRC (self-reference criterion) is very important. The danger is that the marketer (1) will perceive the need in home-country terms or (2) will formulate the message in home-country terms. One good example of a firm's SRC appearing in a promotional message occurred when Pepsodent tried to sell its toothpaste in a Southeast Asian country using the United States as the frame of reference. The firm transferred the "need for white teeth" to the foreign market; however, people in the Asian country chewed betel nuts to achieve the social prestige of darkly stained teeth. Obviously Pepsodent's message was not the appropriate one to persuade these people to buy toothpaste.

Encoding

Once the sender has decided on the message, it must be converted into a communicable form. The message will not necessarily be contained entirely in words. Much of the message will be communicated by way of symbols, colors, body language, situations, and other nonverbal means. As a matter of fact, the Libby company had a very successful international campaign without any words, just a clown pantomiming the enjoyment of eating Libby foods. Obviously, the availability of media will influence the selection of verbal or nonverbal cues. The Libby ad would be less effective in print than television, and certainly impossible for radio.

Most messages will be encoded by way of a combination of verbal and nonverbal methods, so care must be taken to translate not only words but the meaning of symbols, gestures, and body language for proper interpretation by the host culture. For example, producers of menthol cigarettes who wish to communicate a cool image use a lot of green in their advertisements. In tropical countries, however, green represents the jungle and evokes negative images of disease and danger. The Marlboro man is a popular macho image, but consumers in Hong Kong simply could not relate to a cowboy riding around all day in the sun on horseback. Their Marlboro man is still a cowboy, but in Hong Kong he is well-dressed, young, and drives a truck.

Besides changes in these symbols, the context or situation must be considered when encoding a message. A telephone company ran a commercial for Latin American audiences where the wife said to her husband: "Run downstairs and phone Mary. Tell her we'll be a little late." The commercial contained two cultural errors in encoding the message: (1) Latin wives would seldom order their husbands around; and (2) no Latin would feel it necessary to phone to warn of tardiness, since it is expected. Unless all elements of the message are correctly encoded, the receiver will not perceive the message as intended by the sender. Incongruous verbal or nonverbal encoding like the examples given above may distract or confuse the receiver or worse, send an incorrect message.

Message Channel

Much of promotional strategy is concerned with selection of appropriate message channels. As in domestic marketing, the message channel ideally should reach the target market in an efficient and timely manner. For example, print media are less frequently utilized in LDCs where literacy rates are low but are a major message channel in MDCs where literacy rates are high and broadcast commercials are frequently prohibited or heavily regulated. Television is a useful medium in Latin countries where entire families may sit down together to watch. Billboards are suitable in densely populated areas like Mexico City where passerby traffic is high.

A variety of media may be available, but the alternatives and decision criteria regarding other relevant factors will be very different in international communications. Cost and availability of media, literacy rates, ownership of TVs and radios, and other variables will uniquely influence decisions regarding the selection of foreign message channels. For example, low literacy rates in Kenya indicate the use of broadcast media. Of the two, television may initially seem to offer the greatest impact, because it offers a visual, action-oriented approach in addition to sound. However, analysis of TV and radio ownership reveals that while 30,000 Kenyans own televisions, 600,000 have radios. Depending on the target market, radio may offer greater coverage. Other factors such as hours of programming and availability of and scheduling of commercial messages must also be considered in the message channel decision. Usually a combination of channels will be needed to provide the optimum mix of reach and frequency.

Decoding

This stage is analogous to the encoding stage, only on the receiver's end. Decoding refers to the receiver's interpretation of the message sent. The assumption is that for the message to be clearly communicated, the sender and receiver must have the same frame of reference. Since the receiver's frame of reference is fixed, the challenge is for the sender to eliminate the SRC in encoding the message, so that the communications will be in the receiver's frame of reference. Only with the same frame of reference will the receiver interpret the symbols and verbal message as the sender intended.

Translation errors plague the decoding step. Among the many examples of poor translation is the Parker Pen Company's advertisement whose main slogan was "Avoid Embarrassment—Use Parker Pens." With the slogan, the company intended to convey the message that Parker Pens were dependable and would not leak ink. However, the word *embarrassment* was translated into Spanish as *embarazo* which literally means *embarrassment* but is used most often colloquially to mean *pregnancy.* Parker Pen was definitely *not* promoting its pens as contraceptives as some may have thought.[1]

Often the decoding problems are caused by encoding errors. One U.S. swimsuit manufacturer boasted that the wearer could lie in the sun all day and the suit would not fade. The message, when decoded by the Latin American market, was incomprehensible. Why would anyone want to stay out in the fierce Latin American sun all day?

Receiver

By the time the message reaches the receiver, it is likely to be in a somewhat altered form than originally intended. This can result from an accumulation of errors as the message goes through the communications process. (Remember the childhood game where you whispered a phrase to a friend, who whispered it to another friend, and so forth, until a completely altered message returned to the originator?) The sender's SRC may interfere with properly conceiving a message; inadequate knowledge of the culture may lead to incorrect encoding of a message; the choice of message channel might be inappropriate for the message. Cultural differences between the sender and receiver can contribute to faulty decoding and consequently to a confusing message.

In addition, the receiver may not be the one intended. Presumably the message is directed at the prospective consumer, but there is no guarantee that the consumer will receive it. Even if the consumer is exposed to the message, it may be ignored or forgotten. Any of these areas, separately or collectively, will interfere with the intended message. By dissecting the communications process, however, the marketer may be able to isolate problem areas and prevent or quickly correct blunders. Some formal or informal process to promote feedback to help identify problems before they become disasters is an integral part of the communications process.

Feedback

A feedback loop is an important control mechanism for detecting message errors. With a good feedback system a company may be able to correct mistakes in time to save the product. For example, when a major U.S. breakfast cereal company introduced corn flakes to the U.K. they advertised their U.S. package with a cute, red-haired, freckled child on the front. When sales were lower than expected, the company researched the problem and found that children have no role in product selection in the U.K. (unlike the United States). The U.K. consumers could not relate to a child advocating a product. The package was changed and the product successfully reintroduced because the feedback mechanism of the communications process allowed the company to detect the problem in time to correct it. The implementation of a feedback loop can vary in structure from a formal marketing information system which continually monitors a product's progress to an informal system of handling consumer complaints or suggestions. Information can come from consumers, employers, managers, or almost any conceivable source. The key factor is that the feedback information reaches the individual in the company with the authority and inclination to act upon it.

Noise

Surrounding and permeating the communications process is "noise"—the gremlin of the promotional manager. "Noise" is a generic term for any interference with the communications process; it can occur at any stage. Noise can be anything from a doorbell ringing or a dog barking while a message is in progress to competitive advertisements surrounding an ad. No matter what form it takes, noise distracts the consumer (receiver) from the full impact of the message. Noise reduces the effectiveness of the message, but is generally beyond the control of sender or receiver. A dramatic example of noise from competitors occurs in Mexico, where anywhere from 10 to 50 commercials may be heard in one radio station break.[2] All of these messages competing for the listener's attention distract the intended receiver from any one message. Information overload may prevent the listener from remembering the information presented in any one commercial, while selective perception on the part of the listener will provide an automatic screening process which the marketer may find difficult to penetrate.

Advertisers employ a number of techniques to combat noise. Commercials are sometimes aired at a higher volume than programming, though countries like the United States regulate this practice. Creative, eye-catching, interesting, humorous, or dramatic appeals all attempt to break through perceptual barriers. Repetition of commercials will help to reinforce the message in the consumer's mind, as will the use of the same campaign executed in different media.

Understanding the elements of the communications process can improve the marketer's chances of successfully executing a promotional message. By anticipating the possible problems at each stage, the marketer can take action to prevent error and confusion.

EXERCISE 7–1

You can't get there from here—or—How good is your knowledge of geography?

While it is not absolutely necessary in an interdependent world to be able to locate on a map every country in the world, it is nice if you don't omit the island of Hokaido (a major Japanese island) when advertising to the Japanese.

United Airlines did just that in a promotional piece sent to the Japanese announcing the beginning of flight service by United to Japan. In the advertisement was an illustration of Japan sans the island of Hokaido.

Let's test your knowledge of geography. From the list of countries below, select the first and second country due south of the city you are in. Example, if you are in El Paso, Texas, the first country south of you is Mexico and the second country is _____? If you can't find the countries south of you in the list, write them in the space provided.

Mexico	Guatemala
Cuba	Colombia
El Savador	Dominican Republic
Costa Rica	Jamaica
Venezuela	Chile
Brazil	Argentina
Nicaragua	Uruguay
Panama	_____
Honduras	_____
Belize	_____
Peru	_____
Bolivia	_____

Now, go to the nearest atlas and see if you are correct.

THE MESSAGE: THE OBJECT OF THE COMMUNICATION PROCESS

The message is the focal point of the communication process. Unless the message motivates the consumer, he or she will not buy. For that reason it may be the single most important aspect of the promotional campaign.

Adaptation versus Standardization

An important issue in international promotional strategy centers on adapting versus standardizing the promotional campaign as the marketer moves from country to country. If you will recall, we had a similar discussion with regard to adapting or standardizing products, and indeed the two issues are closely related. As with the product-oriented debates, one group recommends customizing advertisements for each country or region because of cultural differences. Their thinking is that the advertising message must relate to consumer motivation. Therefore, since people in different markets buy similar products for significantly different reasons, the advertising message should reflect the appropriate motive for each market. It is with this understanding that the N W Ayer advertising agency varied the Bahamas Tourism campaign throughout Europe. Though most of Europe was exposed to a campaign that emphasized clean water, beaches, and fresh air, the ad in the United Kingdom had a humorous theme and West German ads emphasized the many sports activities offered by the Bahamas. The differences in ads for the U.K. and West Germany reflected different purchase motives in these markets.

There is, however, a fundamental need for the large MNC to be able to control its product and company image for all its markets. In addition, there are substantial economies to be realized, not to mention ease in managing and controlling advertising efforts, if there is only one advertising theme throughout the world. This standardization approach assumes that consumers in various parts of the world will desire the same products for the same reasons, responding similarly to the same promotional campaign. In situations where motives for buying are the same, the most cost-effective approach is standardization.[3]

Neither the standardization camp nor the adaptation camp has had the final word. In fact, it is probably safe to conclude that the consensus among many multinational companies is that there are sufficient cost and control benefits to justify standardizing wherever possible. Yet they also recognize the importance of adapting a promotional message when required by cultural differences.[4] Not surprisingly, a compromise solution to the question of standardization versus adaptation has been developed, called pattern standardization.

Pattern Standardization

Pattern standardization means designing a prototype advertising campaign where the basic theme is expected to be adopted multinationally but which allows for variations in the creative expression of that theme. Thus some attempt at worldwide control is achieved but, where necessary, the peculiarities of the local culture are recognized.

Goodyear International Corporation utilizes pattern standardization in its advertising in Britain and Western Europe. The campaign is designed at the outset for international markets; that is, with transferability in mind. The specific theme or message and all the copy and artwork are developed at the home office. International subsidiaries keep the general framework, the theme, and many of the key components of the campaign but adapt the details to the local market. By doing so the firm keeps a global corporate image, reduces production and creative costs, and gains the global recognition discussed earlier. One of Goodyear's pattern standardization themes was built around Goodyear's success in Grand Prix auto racing and was developed for the European market. Brazil, Mexico, South Africa, Japan, and Australia could exercise local option in deciding whether or not to accept the pattern, and to what degree.[5]

Ford Motor Company's Granada operation in Europe provides another interesting example. Ford of Europe implemented a pattern standardization advertising program in Europe designed to achieve product awareness and to "communicate to each market segment the product attributes the segment perceives as 'fulfilling its needs.' " Marketing researchers began by investigating consumers' perceived needs and perceptions of product attributes across several countries. Prospective new car buyers from Germany, France, the United Kingdom, and Sweden were studied. All countries' consumers responded in virtually the same manner with regard to the importance of "durability." Granada styling scored well in Germany and Sweden, but poorly in Britain and France. The British felt the Granada was safe, but the other countries did not. Sweden felt the Granada to be less reliable than the competition. The Germans wanted "technically advanced" in a car and prefer "smaller" to "average" size; however all countries preferred "average" to "larger" size cars. This information was then utilized to develop a "pattern" for advertising campaigns. For example, "durability" could safely be used in all countries, while variations among countries would be required regarding "safety" or "technical advancement."[6]

In reflecting on the marketing objective of a promotional message, which is to persuade consumers to buy the product by informing them about how the product fulfills their needs, it seems that the mutually exclusive decision to either standardize or modify is an overly simplistic approach. Remember that the bottom line is: Does the advertising communicate a message that is relevant to the market? Whether the sender standardizes or modifies the message sent is only marginally important; it is the message received that must generate sales.

EXERCISE 7–2

Developing a Worldwide Advertising Campaign

The Levi Strauss Company sells Levi's in more than 70 countries. The company is evaluating its present advertising strategy to determine whether to apply a worldwide strategy to all advertising or settle on localized campaigns in each country. Currently, the company creates campaigns locally and regionally. Here are some of the appeals used:

- European television commercials for Levi's are super-sexy in appeal, projecting, in the minds of many at headquarters, an objectionable personality for the brand. These commercials are the result of allowing complete autonomy to a sales region.
- Levi's commercials prepared in most of Latin America (Brazil is an exception) project a far different image than those in Europe. Latin American ads address a family-oriented, Catholic market. However, the quality of the creative work is below the standards set by the company.
- Ads for Britain emphasize Levi's as an American brand. They star an all-American hero, the cowboy, in a fantasy wild West setting.
- In Japan, where an attitude similar to that in Britain exists, local jeans companies had already established themselves as very American. So, when Levi's entered Japan, they positioned themselves against these brands as the "legendary American jeans" with commercials themed "Heroes Wear Levi's," featuring clips of cult figures like James Dean. These commercials increased the awareness level of the Levi name among Japanese consumers from a 35 percent level to a 95 percent level.
- In Brazil consumers are more strongly influenced by fashion trends emanating from Europe than from the United States. Thus, the Brazilian-made commercials filmed in Paris feature young people, cool amidst a wild traffic scene—very French. The theme is "Levi's are favored among young, trend-setting Europeans."

1. Prepare either a defense of the decision to standardize or a defense to adapt to local markets.

2. Assume the decision is made to standardize. Based on the information given above, outline a major theme for a worldwide Levi advertising campaign.

3. Assume the decision is made to compromise between standardization and adaptation with "pattern standardization." Outline a campaign ad using pattern standardization.

PROMOTIONAL STRATEGY

Promotional strategy is a subset of the overall marketing strategy. The tools of the promotional manager include the message and the other elements of the promotional mix. The nature of the market, the nature of the product, and the stages of the product life cycle can all influence how these elements are combined to create a promotional strategy. One well-known author suggests a marketer has categorized the alternative promotional/product strategies for entering international markets.[7] He suggests the following:

Same Product/Same Promotional Message.   As you might imagine, this strategy is followed by very few companies. Though it is quite cost efficient with regard to both production and promotional economies of scale, it is unusual for one product and one message to motivate the world to buy. Coca-Cola and Pepsi-Cola may represent one of the few product types that is truly universal. They satisfy the same need in the same way, for the same reasons, the world over.

Same Product/Change the Promotional Message.   This strategy is more common than the purely standardized approach mentioned above. Though one product may be suited to many markets, international markets by definition are culturally distinct and, as such, often require unique messages to motivate consumers. A good example of this is the Renault 5 car. The car was launched in France with a humorous appeal—an animated cartoon car bouncing down the road with headlight eyes and a bumper smile. In Italy, where consumers are serious about road handling and performance, the Renault 5 was promoted as a comfortable car with good road handling. In Sweden, the message was safety; in Germany, solid construction and gas mileage were emphasized. With this strategy, production economies of scale are still obtained, but promotional costs increase.

Change the Product/Same Message.   The Esso "Put a Tiger in Your Tank" is a classic example of a successful worldwide message. The gasoline had to be changed to meet local driving conditions and local automobile needs, but the same message was translated. In this case, some production economies were lost, but promotional expenses for research, copy, creative work, and so on were one-time costs.

Develop a New Product.   This is sometimes the only viable alternative. As we discussed in the product chapter, many U.S. products are too sophisticated for LDC markets, and products may require simplification or other redesigning to satisfy the needs and wants of the overseas market. A small Utah company, Hart Industries, did just that when it developed a nonelectric dishwasher. The machine is operated by water pressure and may either be a portable unit by attaching it to a faucet or be permanently hooked up to plumbing. It will sell for considerably less than an electric dishwasher and will have a market in both the developing world and the United States.[8] Since new product development has already been discussed in Chapter 4, this is an appropriate time to examine the influence of the product life cycle and the degree of product innovation on international promotional strategy.

PROMOTIONAL STRATEGY AND THE PRODUCT LIFE CYCLE

As you know from Chapter 4, what may be a mature product in the United States may be perceived as an innovation in the international market. Promotional strategy must be adapted accordingly. This section will examine changes in international promotional strategy that may be required as the product moves through the life cycle.

Introduction. In the introductory stage of the product life cycle, the promotional strategy should stimulate *primary demand,* or the demand for the product type. This is particularly important in LDCs where the product may be a *discontinuous innovation.* For example, Gillette is now laying the groundwork in some underdeveloped African countries for what they hope will be a thriving market. They are trying to sell razor blades, but must first sell the idea of shaving. One of their most unique techniques is using a giant shaving brush which is carried from village to village in a van equipped with wash basins, towels, and razors. In a vaudeville-style skit, a volunteer is pasted with shaving cream with the giant brush, and then shaved. Villagers are then invited to try their hand at the fun. This is one of the more unique examples, but Gillette is not alone in its long-term view of new product introduction and promotional stimulation of primary demand.

Personal selling, particularly designed to convince middlemen to carry the product, will be important at this stage. Consumer-oriented promotions may include free samples, cents-off coupons, and informative advertising designed to reach innovators and early adopters. (In the next section we will discuss potential international legal restrictions on these methods.) In international markets, reaching opinion leaders and reference groups may be particularly important in the introduction phase to stimulate adoption of the product.

Growth.   In this stage, sales and profits both begin to take off. *Selective demand,* or demand for a particular brand, is emphasized and advertising becomes more important. Competition will increase during the growth stage of the product life cycle. In international marketing the competition may come from the host country, from other home country firms, or from other country MNCs.

Maturity.   In the United States, when a product reaches the maturity stage of the life cycle, the marketer will attempt to extend the life of the product by developing new uses for the product, by modifying the product ("new and improved"), or by developing new markets. These new markets may include international markets, where the product may once again be in the introduction phase. Tobacco companies in particular are looking to overseas markets as cigarette sales in the United States drop. Competition is heavy at this maturity stage, sales level off, and profits decline due to increased promotional expenditures and price competition. Internationally, care must be taken at this stage; foreign consumers are often less receptive to "new and improved" promotions than are U.S. consumers. Though competition is heavy, many governments prohibit blatantly competitive advertisements. In Germany for example, it is illegal to use comparative terminology: No firm can say its brand is "bettter" or "best." (In comparison, think about how many products in the United States are advertised as being "better" or "the best.")

Decline.   If the company has been successful in extending the product life cycle, this final phase can be delayed indefinitely. Once all alternatives for extension are exhausted, strategic action must be taken. Promotional effort should be cut back at this phase. The product should remain only in the most profitable areas, and be removed from marginal accounts.

Summary

As you can see from the discussion above, promotional strategies in international marketing are the same for each of the stages of the product life cycle as they would be in the U.S. market; that is, in the introductory stage stimulate primary demand, in the growth stage stimulate selective demand, and so on. The problems encountered by the international marketer do not stem from the need to design a different type of strategy for each stage of the product life cycle, but from transferring a strategy designed for one market where the product is in the mature stage of the product life cycle to a market where the product is at a different stage of its life cycle. This was precisely the situation that occurred with the Polaroid Swinger camera, as discussed in Chapter 4. When Polaroid introduced the Swinger to France, the ad campaign used was the same as in the more mature U.S. market. Unfortunately, the Swinger was at the introductory stage in the French market and needed a campaign to stimulate primary demand rather than an appeal appropriate for a mature U.S. market already familiar with the concept of instant cameras.

THE PROMOTIONAL MIX

The promotional mix includes advertising, sales promotions, personal selling, and publicity. The combination of these elements in a coordinated plan to achieve a goal is called a promotional campaign. The composition of the promotional mix depends not only upon the nature of the product and the market (as in the United States), but also upon foreign legal restrictions, media availability, media coverage, costs, and cultural diversity.

Advertising Media

Advertising refers to any *paid* form of a promotional message where the sponsor is identified. This section will examine the various advertising media available in foreign markets with respect to some of the more important international issues facing marketers.

Television.   Television is one of the more highly regulated communication industries. Availability, scheduling, and acceptable products are all regulated to varying degrees by different countries. For example, commercial television is unavailable in Belgium, Denmark, Norway, and Sweden. Holland allows 10 minutes daily of commercial messages; France allows 13 minutes; Switzerland, 15 minutes; Germany, 20 minutes; and Austria, 27 minutes. In Germany, TV scheduling must be arranged by August 30 of the prior year. Many countries prohibit alcohol and tobacco commercials and forbid the use of children in commercials.

Reliable data on audience coverage is always difficult, but is critically important as the rates for television advertising are based on the numbers of viewers in the audience. Costs are usually high for television advertising, but the advertiser can utilize sight and sound and can demonstrate product uses. Most of the heaviest spending television advertisers are MDCs: The top five in expenditures are the United States, Japan, the U.K., West Germany, and Australia. However, for many LDCs like Spain or Brazil, television advertising accounts for more than one half of all advertising expenditures and is an important medium for reaching the entire household.

Satellite transmission has been the cause of recent concern to many countries. Political considerations are beyond the scope of this discussion, but the language problems are considerable to a marketer creating advertisements designed to be transmitted via satellite and which may be received in many different countries. When discussing television regulations, we noted that the internal national advertising regulations vary among European countries. As a result, the International Union of Advertisers Association (IUAA) is urging the European Community (EC) to standardize national restrictions regarding commercials transmitted via direct broadcast satellites.

Radio. Advertising on radio is lower in cost than television, usually covers a smaller geographic area, and relies on sound (words, tone of voice, music, etc.) for impact. Radio is more flexible than other media in that it can reach consumers in their automobiles, homes, places of work, stores, or other locations. However, legal restrictions may also cover radio broadcasters; throughout most of Austria, for example, radio advertising carries a 10 percent tax (posters are taxed 10 to 30 percent; TV ads are taxed 10 percent). Language may be a problem wherever a number of languages are spoken within one listening area. Coverage may also be difficult. In Mexico there are 775 radio stations; 57 in Mexico City alone. Radio covers 83 percent of Mexico and 95 percent of Mexico City, but program ratings are low so that an advertiser must buy a large number of stations and spots. Resulting clutter or "noise" is high; only *two* stations carry programming for as long as 15 to 25 minutes at a time before commercial interruption.

Newspapers. Newspapers have similar problems with coverage. For example Lebanon, with a population of only 1.5 million, has 210 daily or weekly newspapers. Only four have circulations over 10,000, with the average being 3,500. Availability may be a problem with other countries where a lack of paper limits size and frequency of editions. Though newspapers are often the preferred medium for immediacy, some countries like India may require as much as a six-month lead time to place advertisements.

Magazines. Magazines are used somewhat less frequently for international advertising. Though in the United States circulation figures are fairly accurate and magazines can effectively be used to segment the market according to interests and lifestyles, this is not true in most international markets. However, for countries where television or radio advertisements are not allowed, print media comprise nearly all of the advertising budget. Literacy rates are also a consideration when selecting print media. Though the advertisement may be designed to be largely pictorial, few people may purchase the magazine.

One interesting blunder occurred when an advertiser used a pictorial ad, but forgot about how people *read* in the country. The laundry detergent company's ads showed soiled clothes on the left, its box of soap in the middle, and clean clothes on the right. But because people read from right to left in that market, they interpreted the ad as saying the product made clothes dirty!

Other Media. *Cinema* advertising is used quite frequently in international advertising. *Billboards* are used successfully in many countries with high literacy rates, but in other countries they are strictly regulated. *Direct mail* is popular with industrial advertisers, but has problems in countries such as Chile where the receiver is expected to pay one half of the mailing cost. *Trade shows* are an effective way to enter an international market, particularly when marketing industrial goods.

Unique Applications. There are some additional forms of advertising that are unique to some foreign markets. For example, newspapers in some countries sell editorial space; in fact, in Mexico advertisers can even buy space on the front page. In Brazil, advertisers pay soap opera producers to tout their products during the program. Apoio, a Brazilian company that handles advertising for TV Globo, recently signed Ford Motor Company, Quaker Oats, Kellogg, Atari, and General Foods for soap opera spots. For example, on a current 7 P.M. soap opera "Transas e Caretas," leading actor Jose Wilker does "so much merchandising it's amazing he can even remember his lines." He drives a Ford, sells Atari videogames at his electronic store, and plays Pac-Man at home. In one episode the leading character rides his clearly branded bicycle to a well-advertised bank using a new bank card to withdraw money. Having learned that the woman he loves is an imposter, he confronts her friend at a shoe store, pausing in his quest for the truth long enough to ask about a yellow boot. The friend interrupts the confession long enough to explain that the boot is the latest style which all of Brazil will be wearing in the fall. The competitive marketer will want to investigate these more unusual media for advertising opportunities.[9]

Sales Promotions

Cents-off coupons, point-of-purchase displays, samples, and other promotional tools can be an effective tie-in with the advertising campaign. Sales promotions increase in importance in those countries where advertising is heavily regulated, but legal restrictions are also likely to apply to sales promotions. Some countries forbid such promotional tools as samples, free gifts, or cents-off coupons. France forbids sales premiums; no goods can be sold below cost. France also forbids any gift that is conditional upon purchase or a gift that is unrelated to the product; Cracker Jack's famous gift-in-the-box would be illegal in

France. Austria also forbids sales premiums, and Finland forbids use of the word "free" (as in "free gift" or "buy one, get one free"). The American marketing manager must be scrupulously careful to investigate the legal environment in the host country, as many of the marketing techniques commonly used in the United States could be considered illegal business practices abroad.

Personal Selling

Advertising is frequently used in consumer goods marketing when the market is geographically dispersed and consists of many small customers. Personal selling is often applied to industrial sales, where the product is of high unit value and the customers are few and more geographically concentrated.

In international markets the salesperson can be an expatriate (from the home country) or a national (from the host country). An expatriate sales force, though very familiar with the firm and its products, may be unfamiliar with the host country and prone to mistakes caused by their SRC. In addition, an expatriate sales force can be very expensive and difficult to maintain. As a result, nationals are becoming increasingly important in personal selling. They are intimately familiar with the country and may be more readily accepted than a foreigner. The problem, particularly in LDCs, may be the availability of well-educated, well-trained nationals to hire.

SUMMARY

Promotional strategy is an integral component of the overall marketing mix. In international marketing, errors that confuse the promotional message can occur in a number of places in the communications process. The message itself must be carefully selected so as to be meaningful to the foreign market. Selection of media, sales force, or sales promotions will be influenced by the foreign environment and must be carefully planned.

NOTES

1. Oscar S. Cornejo, "Avoid Embarrassment in Latin America," *International Advertiser,* May–June 1981, p. 12.

2. Erika E. Levine, "Commercial Radio in Latin America," *International Advertiser,* January–February 1982, p. 27.

3. "Harvard's Levitt Called Global Marketing Guru," *Advertising Age,* June 25, 1984, p. 49.

4. George J. McNally, "Global Marketing: It's Not Just Possible, It's Imperative," *Business Marketing,* April 1986, pp. 64–70.

5. D. M. Peebles and J. K. Ryans, Jr., *Management of International Advertising* (Boston: Allyn & Bacon, 1984).

6. Michael Calvin, Roger Heeler, and Jim Thorpe, "Developing International Advertising Strategy," *Journal of Marketing,* Fall 1980, pp. 73–74.

7. Warren J. Keegan, "Multinational Product Planning: Strategic Alternatives," *Journal of Marketing,* January 1969, pp. 224–31.

8. "Selling the China Market: It Doesn't Always Take a Lot of Time and Money," *Business International,* February 17, 1984, p. 49.

9. "Brazilian Pitchman," *Advertising Age,* July 2, 1984, p. 24.

CHAPTER EIGHT

Issues in the International Marketing Environment

Up to this point we have examined the "nuts and bolts" of international marketing. We began by discussing the importance of understanding international perspectives in marketing. We reviewed the many aspects of the foreign uncontrollable environment and discussed how those elements might affect marketing planning. Marketing research was examined with an eye to the difficulties encountered in conducting international research. With that information as background, we went on to examine each element of the marketing mix from an international perspective.

Throughout the discussion thus far, we have stressed the importance of understanding and being sensitive to the environment and culture of foreign markets. This chapter will introduce a few topics we consider to be current issues facing international marketers; issues that can have an important impact on the success or failure of international marketing activities. They are important because they pervade all international markets to some extent and, unless properly addressed, can be formidable uncontrollable elements restricting a company's ability to market successfully. Some will be new concepts, but most will be subjects we have alluded to in prior chapters but have not yet discussed in any great depth. To that end, this chapter will provide an overview of some of the key issues and arguments regarding multinational corporations, social responsibility, international business ethics, and trade issues including protectionism, world brands, countertrade, and export trading companies.

MULTINATIONAL CORPORATIONS: MNCs

Who controls multinational corporations? Who should control them? The home country? The host country? The MNC directors? Global agencies similar to the UN? These questions about MNCs have remained unanswered for the past few decades, yet still represent a key issue in international marketing.

The size of MNCs is one factor that causes individuals as well as governments to be concerned about MNC power and control. To illustrate let us look at the financial performance of a few of the world's largest companies. Some of the largest U.S. MNCs, for example, have gross revenues that exceed the gross national product of some countries. In one year General Motors and Exxon reported average gross revenues of $75 billion and $90 billion respectively, outpacing the GNP of Switzerland (averaging $50 billion), Argentina ($44 billion), or Venezuela ($41.2 billion); individually, each company's revenues was greater than the GNPs of Thailand, Chile, and Peru combined. Were we to look at the 100 largest money powers, 39 would be MNCs. Obviously, a great many nations are concerned about the power of these behemoth companies.[1]

How will MNC involvement affect the host country's economy? Many countries have become concerned with this issue of MNC involvement as a matter of hindsight; that is, countries have sometimes realized the extent of MNC investment within their borders only after the MNC has become inextricably entrenched in the local economy. For example, of the 120 largest Belgian companies, 48 are controlled partly or wholly by Americans. American MNCs controlled 90 percent of Europe's production of microcircuits and nearly 40 percent of Canada's manufacturing, mining, and paper industries. However, Americans are not the only owners of multinational corporations; in fact, the relative position of American MNCs has slipped over the past 20 years. In 1963, 67 of the top 100 industrial corporations were U.S. MNCs; in 1979, only 47 were controlled by Americans. Today, some of the 100 largest MNCs originate in Canada, Germany, Japan, France, the U.K., and Italy as well as in NICs, including Brazil and Mexico.[2]

Once a country recognizes the extent of MNC investment within its borders it may react in a number of ways. Some countries have taken drastic measures and have confiscated, expropriated, or nationalized industries (see Chapter 2). This approach was utilized in the past few decades by several Latin American, Middle Eastern, African, and Asian nations, particularly in the communications, energy, and transportation industries. The rationale was that these industries were vital to national defense and could not remain in the hands of foreigners. Other countries, such as Canada, have passed legislation requiring predetermined domestication; that is, MNCs must become involved in the local economy, giving ownership, decision-making power, supply contracts, and management positions to Canadian nationals.

In short, the size, status, and control of multinational corporations is an issue for the 1980s. Nations are concerned about the size of MNCs, their transnational basis of operation, their power, and their control. In turn, MNCs are concerned about the way they are perceived internationally. MNCs have been accused of everything from extending colonialism to exploiting human and natural resources in the name of profit. Do they really deserve this "robber baron" image?

Some would argue that they do not. MNCs in many cases are part of the solution, not part of the problem. This is not philanthropy, but good business sense. For example, MNCs need a healthy, educated work force. One study of more than 200 American MNCs in 12 LDCs reported the following statistics: (1) 9 out of 10 MNCs studied provided free annual medical exams for employees; (2) nearly one half of the companies operate a company clinic, and one fourth have built and operate full-scale hospitals.[3] Most reported that they make their medical personnel available to the local community. For example, in Zimbabwe, Union Carbide operates a 60-bed hospital at Shurugwi with 2 physicians and 18 registered nurses. Several companies sponsor nutrition programs, including Union Carbide which provides free hot lunches in its Egyptian, Kenyan, and Ivory Coast plants. Alcoa Corporation is building a 50-mile-long water supply in order to provide potable water to a mining community in one of their host countries; Sterling Drug company started a blood bank for their local community.

In addition to healthy employees, companies also need an educated workforce. Most multinational corporations try to have as few expatriate U.S. managers as possible. To that end, Sears, IBM, Firestone, and Goodyear all have extensive training programs for national managers. However, they all report that host-country governments often hire away these managers once they have completed training. Sears reported that 44 of its mid-level managers have left the company for positions with locally owned firms; each manager represented 350 man-hours of training. In this indirect way, Sears and the others find themselves helping to improve the local economy. In addition to direct training, some companies support local education for the community. Goodyear and other MNCs provide money for scholarships; IBM lent one of its large computer systems to the University of Karachi (Pakistan). Other companies support adult literacy programs and fund local schools; Union Carbide built and equipped a technical college in Que Que, Zimbabwe, at a cost of $4.5 million, in addition to having built nine other free schools in the country. All of these programs provide a better-educated labor pool for the MNC, but in doing so improve the general educational and health levels of the local populace.

Multinationals also raise the standard of living in host countries by creating wealth. Exports of American MNC goods produced in the host country provide a source of foreign exchange which can be used to buy other needed goods. In addition, MNCs are often involved in building host country infrastructure. In Ghana, a joint-venture aluminum smelter owned by Kaiser Aluminum & Chemical Corp. and Reynolds Metals Co. made possible the construction of a long-sought hydroelectric power project.[4] Caltex Pacific Indonesia estimates that it built nearly 2,600 kilometers of roads at a cost of $100 million, and maintains them at another $1 million annually. Other MNCs have built railroads, ports, docks, and bridges.

Some MNC programs are more philanthropic in nature. Recognizing that their employees are often part-time farmers, MNCs have programs to educate and assist agriculture. In Peru, Carnation has a breeding program designed to increase the quality and production of dairy cows. Chevron has a beekeeping program in Indonesia; Shell supported a porcine breeding program in Asia. MNCs also support local recreation and sports teams, provide land for wildlife sanctuaries, build parks, and support the arts. Goodyear Tire built a mosque near its Indonesian rubber plantations to facilitate religious worship.

MNCs are not in business to do good; they are in business to make a profit, and if they do not make a profit they do not survive. That does not lessen the positive impact of their involvement in LDCs. Bridges, roads, power plants, schools, hospitals, and factories are built in less developed countries by multinational corporations. Is it relevant that the catalyst was entrepreneurship rather than philanthropy?

EXERCISE 8–1

Write a position paper on MNCs. In your paper, try to answer some of these questions. How do you think nations should handle MNCs within their borders? Should they attempt to control the MNC? What if a nation finds itself in the position of many Latin American countries where MNCs control vital industries? How would you respond? How are those situations allowed to happen? Why does the negative image of MNCs seem to overshadow the positive image? What is your "image" of multinational corporations? Imagine yourself as the public relations director for an MNC. What would your goals be? How would you implement them?

SOCIAL RESPONSIBILITY

A number of issues may be discussed under the rubric of MNC social responsibility, but we have selected three topics that we feel are particularly controversial. The first discussion centers on responsibility for introducing innovations to a culture and for the changes that ensue. Can or should an MNC initiate changes in local culture by virtue of technology transfer? A related issue, responsibility for environmental safety including the issue of U.S.-versus-local safety standards is discussed next. The emphasis in this section is upon MNC presence in LDCs and the accused "double standard" with regard to safety requirements. The third issue of MNC social responsibility involves MNC involvement in local politics: Should the MNC be an agent of social change, or by such action is the MNC overstepping its bounds? Our goal in each section is to provide a sample of arguments promulgated on each side of the issue in the hope of generating controversy and discussion. Through such a process you must arrive at your own conclusions.

Responsibility for Innovation

The first ethical issue to be addressed is corporate social responsibility for introducing cultural innovations. We have discussed innovations in the product chapter: the characteristics of an innovation, how an innovation is adopted, "how new is new?" We also discussed diffusion of innovation: How quickly does information about the new product move through society? A question we have not yet discussed is who takes the responsibility for the consequences of introducing an innovation to a society?

An innovation, particularly a discontinuous innovation, can change the behavior and lifestyle of the consumer. Think of the great changes in American society since the advent of the automobile, the telephone, and the computer. These not only had an impact on the use of the horse, letter writing, and arithmetic skills (respectively), but also changed the timbre of life in the United States. Some say the fast pace of today's society and its impersonal nature have been a result. The way we think, the way we learn, the way we communicate and relate to others has changed. Think of the changes that were caused by or influenced by the automobile: more roads, highways, stoplights, traffic jams, air pollution, long commutes to and from work, shopping malls, fast food, drive-through banks and stores, increased distances traveled for vacation or moving residence, mobile homes, car racing, trucking of goods— you can undoubtedly add to this list.[5] The point is to demonstrate not only the enormity of the potential changes, but the exponential growth of all the permutations emanating from one seemingly minor innovation. It is impossible for a marketer to introduce an innovation to a culture with the knowledge that all future consequences have been anticipated. Who then will be responsible? Regardless of whether the consequences are positive or negative, who can take the responsibility for changing a culture?[6]

One of the most unfortunate situations in international marketing provides an unforgettable illustration of the unanticipated repercussions of introducing a seemingly helpful innovation to another culture. During the 1970s the Swiss Company, Nestle, introduced an innovation—powdered baby formula—to Third World countries. The company had identified a need: Babies being breast-fed in these poor countries were often malnourished and starving because their mothers were malnourished themselves. Nestle was convinced that the baby formula would at least provide the infants with essential nutrients. They distributed the formula through maternity wards, clinics, and other channels designed to reach new mothers. Unfortunately, the Nestle company did not anticipate the negative consequences. Many mothers in LDCs are uneducated and pitifully impoverished. They did not understand proper use of the formula and mixed it with unsterilized water. They also tried to "stretch" the formula and diluted the formula too much. Sadly, their infants could not survive on this contaminated, diluted mixture. Even worse, it was later realized that mothers' milk was passing essential antibodies, which were not in the formula, on to the infants. Of course, a mother's milk dried up once her infant was placed on formula, so there was no recourse. This is a tragic example of what can happen when an innovation is introduced to a culture. Nestle now makes all instructions in picture-diagram form for those consumers who cannot read.[7] In 1981 the UN's World Health Organization adopted a set of guidelines for the marketing of infant formula. The code is mandatory for most nations and is legally binding in 23 countries. The Nestle Company abides by the code wherever it markets products.

Responsibility for Safety

On the evening of December 3, 1984, a runaway chemical reaction at a Union Carbide pesticide plant in Bhopal, India, caused a storage tank to erupt, spreading a poisonous cloud of methyl isocyanate gas over the nearby squatter neighborhoods.[8] Within several hours the official count was 1,750 dead, but many estimated the number to be more than double that, in what was termed the world's worst industrial accident. Officials estimated that another 200,000 people were injured, suffering from permanent lung damage. The dead and injured were poor families from the *jhuggis,* or slums, which surround the Union Carbide plant. Most of these people were manual laborers attracted to the area by jobs at the plant.

Predictably after the accident, U.S. lawyers quickly arrived on the scene. Indian lawyers, clerks, and students hired by American attorneys blanketed the shantytowns around the plant, pressing thumbprints of survivors to retainer agreements. Reports of victims retaining as many as six different U.S. attorneys, with agreements they could neither read nor understand, were not unusual.

Plaintiffs contended that the U.S parent, Union Carbide, provided an unsafe design for the Bhopal facility and is liable because it was active in the plant's operation. Carbide asserts that the 50.9 percent owned subsidiary, Union Carbide India Ltd., is a separate business with arm's-length relationships to the parent. Internal documents show that Carbide was considering selling or dismantling the unprofitable Bhopal plant. The parent claims that key safety devices that may have reduced the extent of the damage were either turned off or in disrepair. The company has also suggested that sabotage, not design flaws, may have been the cause of the chemical leak.

Eighteen months later the place of jurisdiction had not even been decided, much less the case itself. The Indian government wanted U.S. involvement, maintaining that the case would flounder in India's overburdened legal system. Union Carbide insisted that the trial be held in India, since the subsidiary is a separate business.

Regardless of the legal outcome of the case, speculation has been rampant. To some the Union Carbide disaster gave fuel to the arguments against MNC involvement in LDCs. Detractors claim that MNCs deliberately build dangerous plants for toxic chemicals outside the home country, in the LDCs. Safety standards, they assert, are below the level necessary to protect the local population. Others claim in defense that the Bhopal plant had adequate safety precautions by U.S. standards; however, the local Indian engineers were not equipped to maintain and repair the safety devices. In addition, once an accident did occur, the local infrastructure was insufficient to prevent disaster; that is, the police department, fire department, ambulances, paramedics, roads, hospitals, and even communications to alert the public were simply not available as they would be in a more developed country. The answer to these questions are important not so much to fix blame, but to determine the chain of events leading to the accident so that a tragedy such as this might be prevented from occurring again.

One thing is certain. The Bhopal tragedy has focused attention on what may be the international policy issue of the 1980s: environmental safety. Heightened awareness has moved environmental control from a technical staff area to a strategic business issue. Previous reliance on engineers and in-house lawyers who simply complied with local regulations has been practically useless as a method of accident protection, and has been too narrow in focus. Companies now recognize that any MNC with a global corporate image to protect is dependent upon public opinion and must broaden the goals of environmental management.

To that end, some MNCs are adopting the concept of product "stewardship": cradle-to-grave responsibility for a product or process, from research and registration through production, promotion, packaging, shipping, and end use. For example, Chevron was among the first to develop a computer-controlled system that provides environmental managers with accurate, up-to-the-minute data on every chemical used in production, where it is stored, and in what amounts, and the name of a contact person. Monsanto now supplies communities with the same detailed information on potential hazards and safety precautions that it provides employees. Plant managers have been instructed to develop community awareness outreach programs including open-house tours and speaking engagements by local executives.

These actions by multinational corporations are indicative of a new commitment to environmental safety. Yet critics claim this is not enough. What should the safety standards for a plant be? Are U.S. standards appropriate worldwide, or yet another example of U.S. "imperialism"? Should MNCs develop one global safety standard? Or, should MNCs set a goal of complying with local rules and regulations?

Multinational Political Involvement: The Case of South Africa

The concept of multinational corporations' direct involvement in host country political situations has been a controversial topic throughout the past decade. Foremost in the controversy, of course, has been the case of South Africa. Throughout the 1980s, governments and international agencies alike have spoken out vociferously against the white supremacist policies of the South African government. Some examples of their explicit actions follow:

- The five countries of the Nordic Council (Denmark, Sweden, Finland, Norway, and Iceland) have endorsed a South African Action Program. Its goal is to reduce, and gradually extinguish, the region's diplomatic, commercial, and cultural ties with the apartheid regime. The program discourages new investment in South Africa, encourages firms trading with South Africa to seek new markets, and pledges to increase assistance to refugees and opponents of apartheid.
- The (U.S.) state of Nebraska has passed a bill making it illegal to invest state funds in any company operating in South Africa that does not comply with the Sullivan Principles.* The state of Connecticut sold stock valued at $4.9 million in 14 companies

---

*The Sullivan Principles is a voluntary, antidiscrimination code of conduct that foreign firms in South Africa follow. Firms are periodically evaluated on how well they comply with the code. For a detailed discussion see "Scouring Corporate Conduct in South Africa," *Fortune,* July 9, 1984, pp. 168–72.

that fail to comply with the Sullivan Principles. A bill passed the U.S. House of Representatives forces firms to comply with the Sullivan Principles and places a ban on new bank loans and computer sales in South Africa.

- Japan does not allow its companies to invest in South Africa nor its banks to make loans there.
- Sweden passed a controversial antiapartheid law making loans to South Africa illegal, prohibiting sale or lease of new equipment without special government authorization, and giving the Swedish government authority to halt technology transfer.
- Canada has revised its antiapartheid code.
- The European Community has changed its voluntary code to be more in line with the U.S. legislation (which is based on the Sullivan Principles).[9]

The United Nations Center on Transnational Corporations (UNCTC) has moved strongly for MNC divestment from South Africa. Their report criticizes the 1,000 MNCs operating in South Africa for failing to support local businessmen in seeking reforms and takes a more aggressive stance for the future. It recommends sanctions including forced divestment for firms that fail to actively push for change. The UNCTC report also demands that MNCs take sides and become actively involved in the internal affairs of South Africa. MNCs that are not part of the solution are part of the problem; CEOs are chastized for not supporting the antiapartheid actions of the local managers. (Note that this is a much more aggressive stance than the previously held position that MNCs in South Africa were only responsible for "cleaning house".)

Despite the recent furor, some MNCs have been active in the antiapartheid movement for over a decade. In 1977 the Reverend Leon Sullivan, a Baptist minister, civil rights leader, and General Motors Corp. director formulated the aforementioned code of corporate conduct. The 125 companies who have pledged to follow the Sullivan Principles (and who pay $1,000 to $7,000 to do so) agree to the following:

1. No segregation of races in any company facility.
2. Equal and fair employment practices.
3. Equal pay for equal work for the same period of time.
4. Training programs to prepare substantial numbers of blacks and other nonwhites for supervisory, administrative, clerical, and technical jobs.
5. A higher number of blacks and nonwhites in management and supervisory positions.
6. Improved quality of employees' lives outside the work environment (housing, schooling, transportation, recreation, and health care).

7. Signatory companies are expected to lobby against the apartheid system.

Companies report annually on their compliance to Arthur D. Little (a Cambridge, Massachusetts, consulting firm), and are inspected by outside auditors. The 1985 (ninth annual) Report showed that the number of signatories had grown over the prior year by 50 percent. Two South African companies—Carlton Paper Corp. Ltd. and Video Vision Enterprise Ltd.—have signed. All but one firm reported desegregated facilities in South Africa, and the number of schools receiving MNC assistance increased by one third to 350. Companies have given $78.5 million to programs supporting black education, health, and training in entrepreneurship. However, of the 285 U.S. companies in South Africa, only half have signed the Sullivan Principles. Of those who have signed, about half are "doing pretty good" according to Rev. Sullivan. Thirty-six companies were rated as "making good progress", including American Cyanamid, American Home Corp., Borden, Inc., Burroughs, Citicorp, Colgate-Palmolive, Control Data Corp., Eastman Kodak, General Motors, Gillette, IBM, Honeywell, Johnson & Johnson, Monsanto, Olin, Pfizir, Sperry, 3M, Xerox, and Union Carbide. General Electric, Carnation, Motorola, and 62 other companies were rated as "making progress."

The issues underlying MNC involvement in South Africa are much the same as those we have described elsewhere: Should MNCs become involved in a country's internal affairs? Many MNCs, like Mobil Oil Corp., prefer not to get involved in confrontational local politics. Or are the American companies, with $2.5 billion in investments, already involved by virtue of their presence? Will divestment, such as Connecticut-based Perkin-Elmer Corp.'s 100 percent sellout, make a strong statement against apartheid? Or by leaving South Africa are these MNCs abandoning the cause and even, coincidentally, harming neighboring nations? General Motors and 3M believe that companies are powerful agents for social change and see U.S. MNCs chipping away at the apartheid regime. The UNCTC says that change is too slow, and the MNCs play into the hands of the establishment. What do you think?

EXERCISE 8–2

Place yourself as the CEO of a major MNC with large holdings in Pretoria, which the company has held since the 1950s. Your firm has not yet signed the Sullivan Principles, and the board of directors is divided as to whether or not to do so. The company is a generous contributor to the local (U.S.) university, but students on campus have been demonstrating against the university's involvement with the company because of the firm's South African investments. How will you address the board at the next meeting with regard to these issues?

INTERNATIONAL BUSINESS ETHICS

Complex ethical problems in international trade often come back to a central issue: Should MNCs adhere to the ethical norms of the home country, the host country, or the international marketplace? The MNC operates in a number of different environments where these ethical beliefs are often in conflict. This section considers two such issues of international business ethics: bribery and counterfeit goods. Again, as in the previous sections, consider the arguments presented here to be representative of those expressed by governments, corporations, and individuals in the global marketplace, but as always come to your own conclusions.

Bribery

- In Mexico, business executives begin a meeting at an expensive restaurant in Mexico City and conclude negotiations on a weekend jaunt to Cancun or Acapulco.
- In Africa, prospective business suitors rent a hotel room in Paris for two weeks, or lend a large car which is never returned.
- One Italian company is building an entire luxury real estate development in Uruguay; no units are for sale to the public, but plots are doled out to favored Latin American officials.
- In Malaysia, business managers invite a minister or other key official to an afternoon of golf, bet heavily, then spend the next three hours swatting the ball into sand traps.
- Japanese businessmen, despite their reputation for competitiveness, sometimes cultivate the art of losing. Discrete executives from the major trading companies may lose as much as $15,000 at games of mah-jongg played with government officials, in a run of "bad luck."

Whether you call it the "black mist" (Japan), a "useful contribution" (Germany), "tea" (East Africa), or "the little envelope" (Italy), most governments feel that a bribe by any other name is still a bribe. The issue in international business centers on the conflict between business ethics and what some may consider the practical necessities of conducting business.[10]

For U.S. businesses, and in fact for MNCs from many other countries, the issue is more than an ethical problem—it is also a legal problem. In 1977 the U.S. Congress passed the Foreign Corrupt Practices Act (FCPA), which makes it illegal for U.S. companies to bribe foreign officials, candidates, or political parties. The FCPA also assesses stiff penalties against executives who have reason to know that their agents are paying bribes, and requires public companies to adopt accounting control procedures to help detect illegal payments. The act provides for fines of up to $1 million for firms not in compliance; company executives, directors, employees, or agents may be fined $10,000 and face five years in prison.[11]

There are, however, different types of bribery recognized by the U.S. government. First, we should distinguish bribery from extortion. Bribery refers to voluntary payments by parties seeking unlawful advantage, whereas extortion refers to payment extracted under duress; both are illegal in the United States. Within the bribery category, one should distinguish between "lubrication" and "subornation." When a relatively small payment or gift is made to a low-level official to facilitate or expedite otherwise legal transactions, this is referred to as lubrication. It is fairly common throughout the world and is not strictly considered a bribe. Under an amended version of the FCPA such small gifts to low-level officials to encourage prompt action are not considered illegal. Subornation, however, is a bribe and is (usually) illegal. It involves a fairly substantial payment frequently not properly accounted for, designed to entice officials to "turn their heads," or to perform an illegal act.

The United States did not have laws against international bribery until 1977. The notorious scandals of the mid-70s naming Lockheed, United Brands, and Gulf Oil (among others) and involving bribes as large as $70 million, brought the bribery issue to national attention and forced Congress to act. Up until that point, publicly held companies involved in illegal payments often found themselves in violation of SEC (Securities and Exchange Commission) or IRS (Internal Revenue Service) rules. As public companies MNCs are required to publicly disclose all disbursements of company funds; needless to say, bribes were seldom revealed.

The subject is a complex ethical issue, in conflict with what many international business experts feel is a way of life in other cultures. Some believe the FCPA places U.S. businesses at a distinct disadvantage, yet most developed countries have laws against bribery as well. For example, West Germany and Italy permit the payment of bribes, but only outside the country. Siemens-AG, a West German electrical manufacturer, allegedly paid bribes to government officials in Australia and Indonesia. Though Siemens was acting within West German laws, bribery is illegal in Australia and Indonesia. Consequently the firm has been charged by the Australian and Indonesian governments with bribery. Even in countries where bribery is tolerated, or in countries like Germany where bribery conducted by Germans in other countries is condoned, whenever top government officials are implicated the consequences are serious. No country officially condones bribery within its own borders.[12]

EXERCISE 8–3

Assume you are an executive of a large multinational firm. While visiting one of your foreign customers, the Minister of Finance for the country made it very clear in a subtle way that your company will have to deposit $1 million in a Swiss account for him if you want to receive a $60 million contract. If you don't, your competitor from a country in Europe will get the contract. If your company gets the contract, it will earn over $12 million in profits. If your company does not get the contract, it will probably have to close a plant and lay off more than 200 employees. Further, the firm will have operating losses instead of profits.

Does the executive have any responsibility to the employees when making this decision? To the shareholders? What should the executive do? What would you do? Be sure to consider all the ramifications when you answer these questions.

Counterfeit Trade

Though trade names and trademarks are protected by law in most developed countries, the makers of "Channel No. 5" or "Chanel No. 6" (the counterfeits) have reason to be concerned. Paris-based Chanel is spending $1.2 million per year and taking 40 to 60 cases to court on charges of counterfeiting. Some of these rip-offs boldly claim right on the bottle's label to be a "good imitation of Chanel No. 5."

Other counterfeiters are not quite so obvious. Recently a number of sources have noted the proliferation of worldwide counterfeits of well-known consumer goods including Levi's jeans, Jordache jeans, Gucci wallets, Louis Vuitton bags, Cartier watches, and even Cabbage Patch dolls. Some of these counterfeiters produce reasonable facsimiles which they pass off as the genuine article. (To foil these imitators, Levi

Strauss now weaves in a microscopic fiber pattern visible only under a special light.) More insidious are the otherwise respectable contractors and jobbers who decide to let their production lines run an extra shift. After closing time, many small factories keep working on "under the table" inventories of the same merchandise.

How big a business is counterfeiting? The U.S. House Energy and Commerce Committee presided over hearings on counterfeit goods and estimates losses from fakes to approach $20 billion a year. The Counterfeit Intelligence Bureau in London says the figure is more like $60 billion a year, but that too is only an estimate. The Commerce Department believes that as many as 750,000 jobs have been lost to imitators.

Who are the counterfeiters? After World War II, Japan used counterfeiting as the first step to economic recovery. Today Taiwan has replaced Japan as the leader in region, with 60 percent of the counterfeit trade. South Korea and Thailand are close behind. Indonesia produces counterfeit auto parts, machine parts, and luxury goods; the Philippines counterfeit sporting goods, luxury goods and apparel; Malaysia, Singapore, and Hong Kong are sources of fake consumer electronics, electronic parts, and apparel. These countries have lax trademark laws and rapidly developing industries. Struggling new businesses have neither the money, the time, nor the inclination to apply for patents. But Southeast Asia is not the only culprit. In Europe, Italy is the villain dealing in counterfeit luxury goods, apparel, and consumer electronics. In Latin America, Brazil and Mexico lead counterfeits in sporting goods and luxury goods. India and Saudi Arabia produce imitation auto parts, electronic parts, and luxury goods; and Canada is the leading counterfeit maker of semiconductors. Not all offenders are foreign: The United States produces 20 percent of the world's fake luxury goods, aircraft parts, machine parts, and electronic parts.

As you are probably beginning to glean from the above discussion, the counterfeit of goods on a global level involves substantially more than a few Members Only jackets or Rolex watches. One manufacturer produced fake parts from stolen Boeing Co. blueprints. Boeing says the parts were pretty good, but the FAA recalled about 30 737s and 727s. SPS Technologies, Inc. says that tens of thousands of "high strength" fastening bolts on commercial and military planes are fakes. Fake parts were found in more than 600 helicopters sold to NATO military and civilian U.S. units, including landing gear assemblies that were sold without heat or stress tests. A U.S. Department of Defense contractor was jailed for supplying fake Boeing and Grumman Corp. parts.

The aerospace industry is not the only industry plagued by counterfeit goods. The American Medical Association says an unknown number of deaths and incidences of paralysis have been caused by fake amphetamines and tranquilizers. The Food and Drug Administration recalled more than 350 intra-aortic pumps used to keep hearts beating during open-heart surgery, due to a fake part.

What can be done? The U.S. passed the Trademark Counterfeiting Act of 1984, which makes counterfeiting a federal crime punishable by a $250,000 fine ($1 million for corporations) and five-year prison terms. In addition, the Tariff and Trade Act of 1985 requires the United States to deny tariff preferences and duty-free imports to LDCs that are havens for counterfeiters. Taiwan passed a law in 1985 that makes trademark infringement punishable by a five-year prison term, and others may follow suit. Some claim that counterfeit trade will move to China, as some Southeast Asian nations get tough. (In China copying is a form of flattery.)

Most firms, like Chanel and Levi Strauss, now rely on their own actions. In fact, the microscopic light-sensitive fiber used by Levi is one example of a $50 million high-tech industry that has sprung up to foil counterfeiters. Ford Motor Company launched a counterattack in 1984, confiscating more than 1 million phony parts in raids and suing the 28 distributors involved. Clearly, counterfeiting of industrial property will be a major issue in the 1980s—and one not easily resolved.[13]

EXERCISE 8–4

As part of its recent strategic move to trade up in the fashion apparel classifications, K mart sends several buyers to Paris, London, and Milan. There they buy 80 examples of the latest fashions straight from the runway. With four- and five-figure price tags these garments are hardly suitable for the typical K mart shopper. The next stop however, is South Korea. K mart intends to sell in its U.S. shops "knocked off" versions of the garments produced in Asia at the express direction of K mart executives. Changes are made in color and fabric; styles are rebuilt and simplified; changes are made to reduce special features cutting costs, and to some degree, quality. K mart therefore is "knocking off" or "emulating" the designs, not copying. Besides, fashion designs aren't protected by the law.

Do you agree that nothing illegal is going on here? Is this business practice ethical? K mart is certainly not alone; in fact most clothing manufacturers follow the same procedure. What would your response be if your employer directed you to take such actions?

TRADE ISSUES

Our final sections are concerned with issues of international trade. The current issues revolving around protectionism, world brands, counter-trade, and export trading companies are present in the following pages.

Protectionism

As we discussed in Chapter 2, all companies in international marketing face trade barriers; the differences are simply a matter of degree and of form. Countries can have a relatively open economy as much of Europe supports, or they can be largely protectionist as Japan and many of the NICs such as Brazil and Mexico. In addition, trade barriers can take on a variety of forms: tariffs, quotas, boycotts, product standards, monetary barriers, and legal barriers to name a few.

The motivations to protect domestic markets are as numerous as the techniques devised to do so. Generally accepted reasons include: (1) protection of infant industry, (2) industrialization of underdeveloped countries, and (3) reasons of national defense. If we think about the first two reasons, it is not surprising to find that the NICs have protectionist policies toward international trade. Most have targeted certain key industries for development and do not want imports from developed economies to inhibit or impair their growth. For example, Mexico and Brazil generally prohibit imports of any goods that are domestically produced. The third reason, national defense, is the rationale for protecting communications, transportation, and energy industries in many countries.[14]

Other reasons are not as defensible. U.S. labor, particularly in mature, competitive industries such as steel and automobiles, cries out against import competition. They want to protect their jobs and their high wages by prohibiting competition from low-wage nations. However, this fear is not supported by an economically valid argument. A Department of Commerce study showed that 90 percent of all U.S. imports come from MDCs, not the low-wage LDCs as alleged. Lower product costs are the result of productivity as well as money wages. Therefore, some may argue that U.S. labor should fight low-priced imports with higher productivity, not with protectionism. In fact, international trade may even provide additional jobs, or ultimately protect domestic jobs by forcing mature industries to remain competitive. Do you think that Chrysler and other auto makers would have modernized if Japanese cars had been eliminated from the market? Conversely, would they have modernized sooner if no protectionism had existed at all?

Other arguments favor protectionism for retaliation. The reasoning is: if the Japanese (for example) enact quotas against us, we'll enact quotas against them. Unfortunately, circular logic of this sort only exacerbates a problem by addressing symptoms and not the essence of the disagreement. Retaliation never recovers the losses caused by trade barriers; in addition, most arguments in favor of protectionist policies are rendered invalid when others retaliate. Protecting the country's standard of living, real wage, or employment are all arguments for protectionism; yet if other nations retaliate, wages, standard of living, and unemployment in the initiating country may in fact worsen.

With recessionary world economies, it is probably realistic for MNCs to expect protectionist policies, at least until economic conditions improve. In the United States, labor unions are primary proponents of protectionism. They are supported by politicians who see an opportunity for popular support, though consumers will eventually pay higher prices and have fewer choices among goods. The United States is not alone in this; trade unions are supporting protectionist policies in many MDCs, including Europe and Scandinavia. Until world economic conditions improve, protectionism and competition will remain an issue for the 1980s.

EXERCISE 8–5

Prepare a position paper on protectionism. In your paper, try to answer the following questions: Imagine yourself the head of the UAW. What goals would you set for the organization? What would be your policy regarding protectionism? Now what if you were the head of Chrysler? Finally, take the viewpoint of yourself, at graduation, buying a brand new car. What then?

World Brands

In Chapter 4 on products and Chapter 7 on promotion we introduced the concept of standardization versus adaptation. We said that strategies for entering global markets could be conceived utilizing combinations of these two alternatives; that is, standardizing both the product and the promotional message, adapting both the product and the promotional message, or standardizing the product (promotion) while adapting the promotion (product).

Presumably products or promotional messages are adapted to better serve the needs of the target market. The marketer may perceive (or determine through marketing research) that the product or promotion in its present form might not be as acceptable to the target member as in a modified form. Sometimes the changes are required by law, but other times the changes are made at the discretion of the marketer. McDonald's, for example, sells beer in its German outlets, wine in France and Spain, and tea in England to conform to the tastes of the local cultures. General Foods sells its Jell-O product in jellied form in Great Britain because that is the way the British are used to seeing it. Pizza Hut, which operates 430 restaurants outside the United States, attributes their success to local management and local flavor. Squid are available on pizzas in Japan, jalapeños in Mexico, bacon in Canada, and low-salt preparations in Korea. Many marketers feel that product attributes such as color, taste, size, packaging, styling, and so forth and promotional features such as the message and its encoding (music, situations, dialogue, attitudes, spokespersons, etc.) should be tailored to local cultures for a marketing plan to be successful.

Other marketers disagree. They cite the benefits of recognizability in reference to what are being labeled "world brands." World brands are products that are basically marketed in the same way the world over. They are the ultimate in standardization. From their inception, they are manufactured, packaged, and positioned the same way globally, regardless of cultural, economic, geographic, or other differences. The major benefits, say their proponents, come from consumers the world over identifying with the same brand.

Why is "recognizability" becoming important? Travel has become easier and less expensive; many more people travel over far greater distances than ever before, and there is no indication that this trend will change. Communications have also undergone tremendous technological leaps during the past few decades linking the globe with communications networks as never before. Satellites allow transmissions of messages through sight and sound the world over; newspapers, magazines, and books travel the world; telephone lines link almost any conceivable points on the globe. These changes have caused a number of consequences for marketers all over the world.

Think of Kodak film, for example. Any tourist, anywhere in the world, will recognize the familiar yellow boxes, will be familiar with the reputation for quality of Kodak film, and will know how to use it. By standardizing the product, consumers anywhere in the world know the brand. In addition, promotional messages will be recognized no matter where they are seen. This is particularly important when communications cross national and cultural boundaries. McDonald's golden arches are seen in 42 different countries around the world, where its 1,625 international restaurants sell 3 million hamburgers every day. Probably the world's best-known trademark, Coca-Cola, is sold in 155 countries in virtually identical fashion.

Look, on the other hand, at Gillette Co. which sells 800 products in more than 200 countries. Its Trac II blades are known in most countries as G-II; Atra blades are called Contour in Europe and Asia. Silkience (hair care products cleverly named from the combination of the words silk and science in the English language) are known as Soyance in France and Sientel in Italy. Gillette recognizes that it is losing out on the recognition factor when, for example, French or Italian advertisements are seen in Germany (where the products are under the Silkience label) or when people travel from one country to another. Some sources say that Gillette may return to "meaningless" brand names (like its Aapri facial scrub) if it intends to introduce world brands.

Other firms take what is essentially a compromise position. Procter & Gamble has successfully marketed such world brands as Camay soap, Crest toothpaste, Head & Shoulders shampoo, and Pampers diapers. P & G strives to keep modifications to a minimum, but recognizes that some adaptations in product or promotion may be necessary. (P & G adapts Crest's taste, Camay's scent, and Head & Shoulders' formula.)

International Playtex, Inc. changed from a strategy of adaptation to a strategy of standardization in a move to streamline its intimate apparel operations. As 50 percent of Playtex intimate apparel sales come from overseas operations, the decision was made to go with a global advertising campaign for its new "WOW" brassiere. New York's Grey Advertising, Inc. was chosen to handle the campaign, a shift from the conventional practice of assigning local managers to hire ad agencies in each country to develop customized campaigns. The central message is the same everywhere—"an underwire bra that still supports yet is comfortable." Three models who have "universal appeal" will appear in all ads. Still, various changes made for local markets will be spliced in later. For example, the French like lacy bras, while Americans prefer more plain, opaque styles. In the United States and South Africa women cannot model bras on TV, so fully clothed models hold bras on hangers. Some commercials are 30 seconds long, others 20 seconds. Some countries want one second of silence at the beginning, others do not. The commercial was filmed in Australia, because Australian TV will only run commercials filmed there. Marketers internationally will be watching the success of the Playtex bra campaign, which has been introduced in 12 different countries.[15]

In another example, a unique advertising campaign for Colgate-Palmolive Company in Britain evolved into a multinational strategy. Switzerland, Austria, and the Netherlands now run the unusual commercial developed by Foote, Cone & Belding which features their Ajax liquid cleaner. The ad's "hook" is a puzzle for the viewer to solve: the Ajax bottle is seen only as a reflection in gleaning bathroom tiles and

faucets. The announcer calls it "xaja diuqil, nomel ro etihw." Six countries now run the ad successfully. Greece was slated for the commercial
until someone realized that "Xaja" means "silly" in Greek.

Most marketers would agree that standardization can provide useful benefits, particularly global recognition. Significant cost savings
can also be obtained through economies of scale in production and
advertising. Marlboro found that the quality of their local advertising
improved when they were able to utilize a global advertising campaign.
Management time and effort is reduced when product managers su-
pervise one coordinated global marketing plan. World brands seem
particularly suited to homogeneous products, such as cigarettes, where
consumer needs are virtually universal and the product can be positioned and promoted in much the same way.

Countertrade

- In 1981, General Electric sold $150 million worth of nuclear
  power plant turbines to Romania. For payment, GE agreed to
  market $150 million of Romanian products through its exten-
  sive global channels.
- A U.S. manufacturer sells machines to China; it is paid in work
  gloves that its own workers use.
- Occidental Petroleum will market Soviet ammonia in a $20
  billion, 20-year contract, in order to guarantee a long-term market for its phosphate fertilizer.

Each of these is an example of countertrade, where some or all of a
payment for goods is made in other goods or services. Countertrade is
a dramatically increasing phenomenon in global trade. One estimate
places current countertrade annual values at nearly one third of the
total $2 trillion of world trade, involving 88 countries. Compare that
to 1972 figures, when only 15 countries required some form of countertrade, valued at less than 2 percent of the total world's trade.

There are several variations of countertrade. Sometimes *barter*
arrangements are simply a swap of goods of presumably equal value.
For example, in 1982 Chrysler Corporation agreed to accept aluminum
from Jamaica in exchange for trucks. A second type of countertrade
involves *buy-back* arrangements where the MDC provides technology
and equipment for a plant, and the LDC pays back in the goods it has
produced. An example of this is the Levi Strauss & Co. arrangement
in Hungary. Levi set up a jeans factory in Hungary, and Hungary
manufactures and markets the jeans for Levi. Sometimes a *clearing-
house* arrangement is set up where a variety of products are exchanged.
This is often done between governments, through the use of trading

companies, or through very large corporations. GE, for example, produces goods in 360 out of the 400 industrial product classifications. With its extensive global marketing system in place, GE found that it could profitably sell Romanian steel products, nails, castings, machine tools, and other construction materials.[16]

Who is involved in countertrade? Governments, trading companies, and large or small corporations are all players. Why? Eastern European countries often seek countertrade because of a lack of hard currency; that is, without some form of "hard" currency such as U.S. dollars, Japanese yen, French or Swiss francs, German deutsche marks, or other readily traded currencies, these countries cannot purchase Western goods (their own currencies are not accepted). As a result, they must trade to get the goods they need from the West. Southeast Asian countries use countertrade to promote exports and to circumvent nontariff barriers. Latin American nations encourage countertrade to maintain the influx of vital imports without damaging their balance of trade. Without countertrade, nations like Mexico and Brazil would have to turn over all export earnings to foreign creditors. This way they can "hide" earnings.

Countertrade is also a way to hide discounts. OPEC nations who cannot get the OPEC-set price for oil but who still wish to sell may agree to accept a favorable countertrade. Sometimes countertrade may be the only way to sell: Indonesia, Malaysia, the Philippines, Thailand, and South Korea all mandate some level of countertrade. Other times barter provides a negotiating edge. When price, technology, and quality are comparable, the winning deal may be the best countertrade. In 1977, Coke beat out Pepsi and won the use of a new Polish bottling facility by agreeing to export 1 million cases of Polish beer. Though marketing an unknown imported beer is quite risky, Coke had two advantages. One, Coca-Cola has been involved in many countertrades before, so had some experience; and two, Coke operates in 155 countries with a marketing system more extensive than probably any other U.S. firm. The beer was sold in the U.S. Midwest successfully under the name *Krakus*.

Of course, countertrade is not all positive. Barter can add anywhere from 2 to 12 percent to the cost of a deal. Some companies do not know which products to choose. GTE Corporation is still wondering what to do with the pink and orange telephone rotaries it received from Poland in exchange for telecommunications equipment. McDonnell Douglas is still trying to market Polish sausage and hams, and Caterpillar Tractor served Algerian wine in its company cafeteria for years, after an unsuccessful countertrade. Coca-Cola's biggest countertrade was for its Yugoslavian wine, Slovin. As Coke's former financial officer was quoted as saying: "The wine was terrible, the bottle was terrible, and the label was terrible." Coke brought in an enologist to change the Yugoslavian processing; found an Italian firm to redo the label; and sells the wine as *Avia* for as little as $1.98 per bottle in the United States. (Avia is now being test-marketed in Japan.) Obviously, countertrade deals are not for the weak of heart.

To prevent such fiascos, many firms and government agencies employed third-party trading companies such as Philipp Brothers or Mitsubishi. The U.S. Department of Commerce also offers assistance to U.S. exporters. Congress has recognized the importance of international trade and countertrade and has acted to facilitate the entry of U.S. companies into global markets. As you read the next section on the new U.S. export trading companies, you may want to be pondering your potential future involvement in world trade. Do you think the ETCs are the answer to U.S. trade imbalance? Would you be interested in being employed with a trading company? Why?

Export Trading Companies

International trade is believed by many economists to be one of the most important factors for economic health. The United States enjoyed an international trade surplus for nearly a century, from 1888 until 1971. Since 1971 however, the U.S. trade deficit has increased steadily. By 1982, the total trade deficit was $43 billion, nearly $32 billion of that in merchandise trade deficit. In 1983 imports increased by $16 billion while exports decreased by $10 billion, bringing the trade deficit to $69 billion. By 1984 the trade deficit surpassed $100 billion and continued its rise throughout 1985 and 1986.

The reasons offered for this trend are many. Some economists feel the strength of the U.S. dollar during the first half of the 1980s was the culprit, causing U.S. exports to be priced out of some international markets. The global recession in the early 1980s is also cited, which caused many countries to decrease spending on imports. The U.S. economy was the first to recover in 1984, so U.S. imports increased accordingly while other countries were still restricting their buying. Third World debt also limits markets for U.S. goods; the IMF and other creditors have imposed austerity programs to induce LDCs to increase their exports and decrease their imports. All of these factors are detrimental to the U.S. trade balance.

To create new opportunities for American businesses to compete in international markets Congress passed the Export Trading Company Act of 1982 (ETC Act). Its goal is to encourage the development of U.S. export trading companies, particularly for the benefit of small and medium-sized companies who have not explored their export potential.

In fact, most small or medium-sized firms are essentially nonparticipants in export trade—85 percent of U.S. exports come from 250 firms; 25 percent of exports come from only 50 companies. These are the large MNCs, listed as some of Fortune 500's major corporations. Congress believes there are some 20,000 additional smaller firms which produce goods that could be competitive in global markets, but which do not export because of a lack of financing, experience, expertise, and confidence.

The act defines an export trading company (ETC) as a person or association (partnership, corporation, etc.) which is in business principally for exporting. The test is that more than 50 percent of the ETC's revenues be export-related. The following functions are permitted to be offered by an ETC:

- Consulting.
- International marketing research.
- Advertising.
- Product research and design.
- Insurance.
- Selling.
- Legal assistance.
- Distribution.
- Trade documentation.
- Freight forwarding.
- Communication.
- Warehousing.
- Foreign exchange.
- Taking title.

Of course not all ETCs provide all of the above services, nor must they. In addition, ETCs can arrange for financing through the Export-Import (Eximbank) ETC loan guarantee program.

The unique feature of the ETC Act is that it amends prior legislation in two key areas: banking and antitrust. It amends the Bank Holding Company Act and permits banks and banking entities to invest in ETCs. (They were not previously allowed to invest in export companies.) This gives ETCs greater access to financing. The ETC Act also clarifies the jurisdictional reach of the Sherman Antitrust Act and of the Federal Trade commission in export commerce. It provides for issuance of "export trade certificates of review" under which the export-related activities of the ETC receive specific antitrust protection. This allows businesses to be certain that if they collaborate to trade internationally they will not face litigation brought by the government, as long as their conduct does not have a "direct, substantial, and reasonably foreseeable effect" on domestic commerce.[17]

By the mid-1980s about 45 companies had formed export trading companies, with mixed results. Many have found that American businesspeople simply do not feel "ready" to move internationally: They fear the unknown. Most have realized that the economic conditions contributing to the U.S. balance of trade deficit, including the strong dollar, sluggish global recovery after a serious recession, and Third-World debt, have not greatly improved. Though the ETC Act offers some provisions to make trade easier, it is not enough to overcome the economic barriers.

Sears was one of the first and largest to move, forming Sears World Trade in 1982. Its promotional literature claimed "we are a global trading company, the first of its size, scope, and independence in the United States. Sears World Trade offers a complete portfolio of capabilities in the areas of trading, trade finance, and business consulting."[18] Sears had hoped to take advantage of its extensive global channels. As the world's largest retailer, Sears's international buying and distributing operations should have provided it with a strong network for entry into global trade. However, by April 1984 Sears World Trade (SWT) had lost $16 million on revenues of $100 million, and its chairman, Roderick M. Hills, resigned. Sears is currently reevaluating the unit. Perhaps new management will be able to turn SWT into a world trading company as intended. However, as a recent article in *The Wall Street Journal* reported, almost no ETCs are currently making money, and most have negotiated only a handful of deals.[19]

The U.S. trading companies are patterned after the *sogo shosha,* or Japanese trading companies, which have had an illustrious past but may also face an uncertain future. The 16 "general trading companies" in Japan, of which Mitsubishi Corp. and Mitsui and Co. Ltd., may be the most well known, perform a wide variety of functions. They buy and sell on world markets, act as intermediaries in third-party deals, perform marketing research, consult, finance trade, and generally profit from their considerable connections around the world. In recent years, however, the *sogo shosha* have averaged less than 5 percent return on equity, and their net profit on sales is less than 0.1 percent. Like the U.S. ETCs, they are finding that the large manufacturing and service companies have in-house trading departments or have entered international joint ventures and no longer require their services.

NOTES

1. Frank P. Popoff, "Planning the Multinational's Future," *Business Horizons,* March/April 1984, pp. 64–68.

2. R. Beeman and S. Timmins, "Who Are the Villains in International Business?" *Business Horizons,* September/October 1982, pp. 7–10.

3. Ann M. Micou, "The Invisible Hand at Work in Developing Countries," *Across the Board,* March 1985, pp. 8–17.

4. Joani Nelson-Horchler, "U.S. Multinationals: Benefactors or Bandits?" in Phillip D. Grubb et al., *The Multinational in Transition,* 2nd ed. (Princeton: Darwin Press, 1984), pp. 393–402.

5. Lee A. Tavis, "Multinational as Foreign Agents of Change in the Third World," *Business Horizons,* September/October 1983, p. 48.

6. George W. Coombe, Jr., "Multinational Codes of Conduct and Corporate Accountability: New Opportunities for Corporate Counsel," in Grubb, *The Multinational in Transition,* pp. 424–56.

7. "Several Organizations Are Entertaining Steps on Product Safety," *Business International,* June 1, 1984, p. 171.

8. *The Wall Street Journal,* May 1, 1986, p. 16.

9. *Business International,* February 22, 1985, p. 63.

10. Jack G. Kaikat and Wayne H. Label, "American Bribery Legislation: An Obstacle to International Marketing," *Journal of Marketing,* Fall 1980, pp. 38–43.

11. "The FCPA Revisited: What Companies Should Know to Soften Its Impact," *Business International,* June 1, 1984, pp. 173–74.

12. Brooks Jackson, "Overseas Bribery Gets a Lot Less Attention after Cutbacks by the Justice Department," *The Wall Street Journal,* February 22, 1983, p. 3.

13. *Business Week,* December 16, 1985, pp. 19–27.

14. Dora M. Khambata, "Protectionism: The Dismal Future of World Trade," in Grubb, *The Multinational in Transition.*

15. "The Counterfeit Trade," *Business Week,* December 16, 1985, pp. 64–72.

16. "Straight Cash for Goods? No Longer a Sure Bet," *American Import/Export Management,* October 1983, pp. 36–44.

17. *Export Trading Company Guidebook,* Department of Commerce, March 1984.

18. John W. Dizard, "Sears' Humbled Trading Empire," *Fortune,* June 25, 1984, pp. 71–75.

19. "Export Trading Firms in U.S. Are Failing to Fulfill Promise," *The Wall Street Journal,* May 24, 1984, p. 1.

Glossary of International Terms

Ad valorem tariff, tax or duty: A tax imposed by the customs authority of a country that is based on the value of goods imported.

Agency for International Development (AID):   An agency of the U.S. government that administers U.S. economic and defense aid programs to developing countries.

Arbitration clause: An agreement in a contract between a buyer and seller that contractual disputes will be settled by a third party (an arbitrator) rather than by litigation.

Antiboycott law: A U.S. law prohibiting U.S. companies from participating in Arab countries' boycott of Israel.

Balance of payments (BOP):   A country's financial statement that reports on the total value of payments for all goods, services, and money by the residents of one country with the residents of all other countries of the world during a specific time, generally one year. When the value of payments paid to citizens of other countries is greater than the value of payments received, the BOP is in deficit.

Balance of trade: The relationship between the total value of a country's merchandise trade of imports and exports. A country's balance of trade is only one aspect of its balance of payments.

Barter: Trade in which merchandise is exchanged directly for other merchandise without use of money. Barter is one type of countertrade.

Cartel: A group of suppliers that controls the supply and price of a product or commodity. OPEC (Organization of Petroleum Exporting Countries) is one of the better-known cartels.

Central bank: The principal agency that controls a nation's monetary holdings. If a country requires exchange permits, the central bank is the agency most often responsible for issuing them.

Code law: The foundation for a country's legal system that has specific written rules (codes) of law. Under code law, the legal system is generally divided into three separate codes: commercial, civil, and criminal.

Common law: The foundation of a country's legal system that is based on tradition, common practice, and legal precedents set by the courts through interpretation of statutes and past rulings. England and most of her former colonies have common law as the basis of their legal systems.

Confiscation: Seizure of foreign-owned assets by a government without compensation.

Convertible currencies: A nation's currency that can be easily exchanged for other currencies.

Counterpurchase: A type of countertrade where the seller agrees to sell a product at a set price to a buyer and receives payment in cash. However, the first contract is contingent on a second contract which is an agreement by the original seller to buy goods from the buyer for the total monetary amount involved in the first contract or for a set percentage of that amount.

Countertrade: Payment by a customer entirely or partially in goods or services. The types of countertrade are: barter, compensation deal, counterpurchase, and buy-back.

Countervailing duties: Additional tariffs levied on an imported good that the importing country rules has benefited from subsidies in production, exporting, or transport.

Currency exchange controls: A government controls the exchange rate between its currency units and the currency units of other countries.

Discretionary changes: Refers to marketing changes an international marketer has the option to make. Such changes generally reflect cultural needs but are optional for product or other marketing-mix adaptations.

Domestication: The gradual transfer of a foreigner's assets to nationals. This can be government initiated or it can be a strategy followed by a company to forestall expropriation.

Dumping: Selling goods in a country below total cost of production. Can also be interpreted as selling goods in a country at a price substantially lower than in the home market. Mainly an issue when the receiving country considers the activity detrimental to local industry. The importing country may apply countervailing duties when goods are dumped.

Devaluation: The official lowering of the value of one country's currency in terms of one or more foreign currencies. Thus, if the U.S. dollar is devalued in relation to the French franc, one dollar will "buy" fewer francs than before.

Duty: A tax imposed on imports by the customs authority of a country. Duties are generally based on the value of the goods (ad valorem duties), some other factor such as weight or quantity (specific duties), or a combination of value and other factors (compound duties).

EC (EEC): The European Community. Originally called the European Economic Community (EEC).

Exchange rate: The price of one currency in terms of another, that is, the number of units of one currency that may be exchanged for one unit of another currency.

Expropriation: Seizure of the assets of a foreign firm by a foreign government with appropriate compensation.

Foreign Corrupt Practices Act (FCPA): A U.S. act passed in 1977 which imposes stiff fines and jail sentences for U.S. corporations and executives convicted of international bribery.

Foreign exchange: The currency or credit instruments of a foreign country. Also, transactions involving purchase and/or sale of currencies.

Free trade zone: See **Foreign trade zones.**

Foreign trade zones (FTZ): Areas designated by the government of a country for duty-free entry of goods. Merchandise may be stored, displayed, used for manufacturing, and so on within the zone and reexported without duties being paid. Duties are imposed on the merchandise (or items manufactured from the merchandise) only when the goods pass from the zone into an area of the country subject to customs (tariffs) duties.

Foreign freight forwarder (freight forwarder): An agent that handles export shipments for compensation. A foreign freight forwarder is among the best sources of information and assistance on U.S. export regulations and documentation, shipping methods, and foreign import regulations.

GATT (General Agreement on Trade and Tariffs): An agreement among more than 90 countries to eliminate discriminatory trade practices. Attempts to eliminate unreasonable import duties, nontariff duties, and other trade barriers.

Gross domestic product (GDP): The market value of a country's output of goods and services produced in the country.

Gross national product (GNP): The market value of all a country's goods and services produced and investment and interest income earned in the country and abroad in a specified period of time, usually one year.

Hard currency: A country's currency that is easily exchanged into other currencies. The U.S. dollar, French franc, and English pound are examples of hard currencies.

IMF: The International Monetary Fund was formed after World War II by the governments of some of the Allied powers as a part of the Bretton Woods international monetary system; (two other elements of this system were GATT and the IBRD or World Bank). The objective of the IMF was to stabilize foreign exchange rates and to help establish freely convertible currencies. Today the IMF's primary role is providing short-term liquidity to countries with balance of payment problems (for example, Brazil and Argentina).

Infrastructure: Such basic attributes of an economy as roads, railroads, communications, water and sewer systems, energy, and so on. Sometimes used to refer to the basic foundation required for any economic activity to be able to operate and prosper. For example, the infrastructure of business would include a distribution system, banking, media for promotion, and so forth.

Letter of credit: A document, issued by a bank per instructions by a buyer of goods, authorizing the seller to draw a specified sum of money under specified terms, usually the receipt by the bank of certain documents within a given time.

Mandatory changes: Refers to marketing changes an international marketer must make in order to comply with a country's laws, standards, and other requirements.

Nationalization: Government takeover and operation of private property.

Organization of Petroleum Exporting Countries (OPEC):   A cartel of oil producing countries whose purpose is to control the world price of oil.

Organization for Economic Cooperation and Development (OECD):   A worldwide organization made up primarily of industrialized countries of the West. The OECD publishes a bimonthly report of economic indicators for member countries (*General Statistics*) as well as special studies on many other topics.

Price escalation: Increase in price of exports resulting from additional costs of transportation, packing, tariffs, insurance, and increased number of middlemen.

Quota: The quantity of goods of a specific kind that a country will permit to be imported without restriction or imposition of additional duties.

Sogo sosha: The Japanese name for a general trading company.

Tariff: See **duty.**

Trading company: International business that trades (buys and sells) goods between nations. They buy and sell, accumulate, transport, and distribute goods from many countries.

UNESCO: United Nations Educational, Scientific and Cultural Organization.

World Bank: Formed after World War II as the IBRD (International Bank for Reconstruction and Development), the World Bank is a part of the Bretton Woods international monetary system (see **IMF**), designed to provide long-term capital to aid economic development.

WHO: World Health Organization, a United Nations agency concerned with such areas as pharmaceuticals, food and nutrition, hospitals, and other health-related issues.

Glossary of Middlemen Institutions

DOMESTIC AGENT MIDDLEMEN

1. *Manufacturer's export agents (MEAs)* have a short-term, largely sales-oriented relationship with the manufacturer. Where a firm would have one EMC that operated as its marketing department, it would employ several MEAs as all or part of a sales force but doing business in their own name. The MEAs also work on a straight commission basis, but in more limited geographic markets than EMCs.

2. *Brokers* bring small buyers and small sellers together on a low-cost, deal-by-deal basis. Brokers may specialize in commodities or by country. The food industry frequently utilizes food brokers which are an example of commodity specialization. On the other hand, Satra Corporation in New York specializes in Soviet Bloc (country specialization) deals. A marketer might choose either type of broker when the firm has seasonal business or when business is to be transacted on a one-time basis.

3. *Selling groups* represent firms that join together to export as a group rather than export individually. When done on a commission basis, this is considered an agency relationship, known as Webb-Pomerene Export Associations (WPEAs). The Webb-Pomerene Export Trade Act of 1918 enabled firms to join forces when exporting, providing there were no consequences that would reduce domestic competition. The WPEAs act in varying capacities ranging from agency-type services such as advertising and promotion to full merchant wholesaling and marketing functions.

4. *Buying offices,* in contrast, work for the buyer rather than the seller. They generally specialize by product type and often provide a good source of business for the seller. They are not an appropriate

channel for a firm seeking a continuing relationship in international markets, but a buying office may in fact continue to buy from the same seller over a number of years. The key disadvantage is that the seller's role is essentially passive.

DOMESTIC MERCHANT MIDDLEMEN

1. *Export merchants* are essentially domestic merchant whole-salers operating internationally. That is, they purchase goods from a number of manufacturers and fill orders from foreign sources. Most specialize to some degree, usually along product lines such as industrial goods or consumer goods. They may carry competing lines and main-tain no particular loyalty to any specific manufacturers, but support the best-selling lines.

2. *Export jobbers* are analogous to the domestic drop shipper who arranges to buy goods domestically and then resells them to foreign buyers without ever taking physical possession of the goods. They do however, take title. Export jobbers therefore deal in bulky goods such as raw materials, which they arrange to ship directly from producer to end user.

3. *Export buyers* deal in distressed merchandise, in overproduction, or in obsolete goods which they purchase at reduced prices for sale overseas. They do not represent a major force in international distri-bution, but are mentioned in the interest of completeness.

4. *Foreign importers* may have offices in the manufacturer's home country which facilitate international sales for firms seeking a low level of foreign involvement. These foreign importers buy goods for resale in their home country.

FOREIGN AGENT MIDDLEMEN

1. *Manufacturer's representatives* may be called sales agents, res-ident sales agents, exclusive agents, commission agents, or indent agents. Regardless of the name, they usually cover a limited geographic area for the firm; that is, they may be responsible for a city, a region, a country, or even several countries. Manufacturer's representatives basically function as field sales representatives. They do not handle credit, market risk, exchanges, shipping, or handling, nor do they take physical possession of the goods. Essentially they act as part of the firm's sales force. When well chosen, well motivated, and well trained, they can provide excellent market coverage while still providing the manufacturer with control.

2. *Brokers,* like export brokers, bring buyers and sellers together (particularly in the commodities and food industries). Also like export brokers, they are paid by commission on a deal-by-deal basis.

3. *Factors* perform all of the normal brokerage functions, but also finance the sales transaction. Their fee for service is commensurately higher than brokers to cover the cost of financing.

4. *Managing agents* conduct business with foreign governments, under exclusive agreements with the parent company. Not strictly "employees," managing agents may even invest in the deal themselves.

FOREIGN MERCHANT MIDDLEMEN

1. *Distributors* often have an exclusive contract with the manufacturer to distribute the product. If their business relationship is a good one (i.e., profitable for both) the manufacturer may still retain a good degree of control. A good distributor will in turn want to comply with the wishes of a successful manufacturer in order to maintain the contract.

2. *Dealers* perform a function similar to distributors, but generally sell industrial goods or consumer durables. As in domestic markets, dealers are found in truck, tractor, and automotive industries internationally.

3. *Import jobbers* purchase goods directly from the manufacturer and sell to wholesalers, retailers, and industrial buyers. The import jobber is also known as an import house or an import merchant.

4. *Wholesalers and retailers* import for their own outlets and for redistribution to smaller middlemen. The combination retailer-wholesaler is more important in foreign countries than in the United States, and it is not uncommon internationally to have the large retailers selling to smaller retail stores.

INDEX

*This book has been set on Penta, in 10 point
Century Schoolbook, leaded 2 points. Chapter
numbers and titles are 12 point Century
Schoolbook. The size of the type page is 27
picas by 47 picas.*